"The best audience for Balducci's book might be those who are most unlike her—people with one child, or people with daughters. Or even people who have no children, but are curious about those who do.

"Balducci is, first and foremost, a reporter, recounting the internal workings of a family that includes five children, all of them boys. She watches them—and herself—carefully, and remains humble before the truth of her (earthy) experience. She loves the world she inhabits, but includes no strident advocacy in her account of it, relying instead on gentle revelation and a generous dose of humor."

—**Matthew Lickona**, author, *Swimming with Scapulars: True Confessions of a Young Catholic*

"With wit and insight, author and supermom Rachel Balducci gives readers a peek into living life in a home filled with boys. Funny, heartwarming, edifying, and always uplifting, Rachel shares her joy for parenting in a way that will inspire you to be a better wife and mom. Rachel Balducci is the 'cool mom,' the best friend, and the confidante you are looking for when things start to get a little crazy around your home. She teaches us that family life, with all of its ups and downs, is truly one of life's greatest gifts."

—**Lisa M. Hendey**, author, *The Handbook for Catholic Moms*; founder, CatholicMom.com

Raising Boys Is a Full-Contact Sport

Raising Boys Is a Full-Contact Sport

RACHEL BALDUCCI

SPIRE

© 2010 by Rachel Balducci

Published by Revell
a division of Baker Publishing Group
P.O. Box 6287, Grand Rapids, MI 49516-6287
www.revellbooks.com

Spire edition published 2012
Previously published under the title *How Do You Tuck in a Superhero?*
ISBN 978-0-8007-8826-1

Printed in the United States of America

12   13   14   15   16   17   18   7   6   5   4   3   2   1

To Paul Vincent
and our boys
For filling my days with adventure, joy,
and overwhelming amounts of love

And to
Steve and Karen Swenson
Whose dedication as parents taught me
the importance of family in the first place

Contents

Introduction

The Grass Is Always Greener

It is the fortieth anniversary of my mom and dad's wedding. My siblings and I have decided to celebrate with a party. We will be inviting a few hundred of their closest friends, and because it is spring, we are having the party in my backyard.

My backyard. The one I use to corral my five sons.

The thing about my backyard is, it's very proud of its heritage. My grass screams at the top of its botanical lungs that BOYS LIVE HERE, and you'd better not forget it.

How can I forget it, is what I'd like to know. Seriously, I ask myself this question nearly every single day. How, I wonder aloud, can I mask the reality of my life? It's not that I want to hide the fact that I have boys, but some days it would be nice not to have the lawn advertise our genetics.

One evening as I walked around my yard to prepare for the party, I made note of the state of things. There are bald spots in the grass—I don't know the exact number because there are so many spots that I'm inclined to just count the grass instead. There is a giant mound of dirt in one corner of the yard, where the boys go to mine for treasure or dig to China. There is a lovely birdfeeder attached to the garage—it hangs at waist level and gives the impression it is for the boys' avian enjoyment. Really, I put it that low to cover a giant hole created by an arrow gone terribly astray.

Yes, this yard is home to flying projectiles and sailing basketballs and whirling baseballs. It hosts soccer games and bonfires and the occasional bocce tournament.

This yard has been "rode hard and put up wet." It screams *boy*, and that is a difficult sound to drown out.

You can tell a bunch of boys live here. It's not that we display the Jolly Roger or post Beware signs on the front gate. We don't even have a rope swing coming off an upstairs window—though my boys have been drawing up plans for one. It's all because of our yard.

I remember a conversation I had with a friend who has one child, a precious little boy who was then approaching toddlerhood.

"Yes," she admitted, somewhat embarrassed, "there is now a bald spot in the sod where we caught him digging. The hole is almost the size of a quarter!" And I'll tell you right now, that sentence moved me to tears, on so many levels. Could a hole really be only the size of a quarter? I've never seen one that small. And only one hole? How very curious. And sod—what is this thing of which you speak?

Of course, I'm painfully aware of what sod is, how I don't have any, and how I'd really like some. I think all it would take is some lush greens to make me forget every one of my cares in this world.

Unfortunately, my husband has no interest in investing in something that will be gone (but not forgotten) in a matter of months. Have you seen, he'll ask me, how our boys behave outside? Are you fully aware of their tunneling capabilities?

It's true those boys can dig. It's quite impressive, actually. Our boys are some of the most ardent digging machines I

12

have ever seen. If you give them a shovel, they will seek out dirt and excavate before you can say Mike Mulligan.

For a while, when the boys were very little, the digging didn't bother me. I would send them into the backyard, and if they asked for a shovel, I would generously oblige. My rules were simple: 1) everyone must be wearing closed-toed shoes, and 2) no one is to take out his frustration with shovel in hand. While I agree that a lizard's tail does indeed grow back, I'd rather not find out if the same would be true of your brother's finger.

Off they would go, my precious little boys, to spend hours shoveling and exploring across the yard. I would feel slightly bad on those evenings when my husband would arrive home from work after dark and be forced to navigate through a field of divot land mines.

"This is a bad idea," he would say, rubbing his ankle while leaning against the kitchen wall. "It's dangerous. And our yard is going to look terrible."

"It's fine," I would say, and then tease him for being so uptight. "What boy doesn't like to dig?" I'd ask, and then I'd remind my husband that he probably did the same thing when he was a boy.

The thing about the digging was, it bought me time—precious, much-needed time, with those boys outside and not in the house literally climbing up the walls. For each hole they dug in the yard, I got thirty minutes of blissful quiet inside.

But now a few years have passed. We are all older and I'm a little wiser. And I want a nice lawn. I'm greedy that way. What's so wrong, I'll ask my husband, with wanting things to look beautiful out there? Nothing, he will tell me, except for that tiny detail of your having five boys who are in the habit of digging.

I understand this is not necessarily mutually exclusive; a person can give birth to a bunch of boys and still have a lovely yard. And I do make efforts to beautify what we have. Slowly, I'm building up a nice collection of potted plants and climbing vines and gorgeous hanging baskets around the house. I've even added some Tuscan-themed ironwork to the outside of the garage.

It's just . . . I want more—more beauty, more elegance, and mostly, more grass.

1

Proper Care and Feeding

Through the Stomach

My boys' love language is food—they love food, and when I buy food they feel loved by me.

One Saturday morning I was headed out to the giant food warehouse club and invited my ten-year-old son, Elliott, to come along. It was like the hottest date he will ever go on in his life.

"What are you getting?" he asked. I explained that I had a list of things to buy, but that he could also pick out some things as well. I am throwing in the towel when it comes to all natural all the time. A few years ago I tried shopping only the perimeter of the grocery store. It didn't go over too well.

Nothing says I love you like processed food.

When we arrived at the store, my son was almost moved to tears. The sight of a forty-eight-pack of hot dogs left him speechless. His jaw dropped as I heaved a family-size box of waffles into our cart. The beauty of it was almost more than he could bear.

We had a great time together that morning, and daily living was storybook perfect while the larders were full.

I have started to notice a trend—on the days when I've grocery shopped and the boys come home to a stocked pantry and fridge, there is something in the air. It's an excitement, a *glee*, that I don't see on any other occasion. Christmas comes close, but it's hard to compete with a ten-pound bucket of chocolate milk mix.

"You went shopping?" they will ask, and when I nod my head yes, they run over and tackle me with joy. It's not just about having food in the house—it's about having lots and lots of food. So much that it practically spills out of the refrigerator when you open the door.

That, my friend, is living the good life.

At first I didn't understand the concept. But at some point it just came to me—this is how my boys feel loved. The way to a man's heart is indeed through his stomach. A mom with boys came up with that saying.

The downside to all of this is that the more food there is, the more my boys will eat. If I have purchased hot dogs and Hot Pockets and a sleeve of peanut butter crackers, my boys want it all. They eat those things, and then wonder aloud what's for snack.

I do understand the concept of moderation, that idea of telling my boys no, you've had enough. But the minute I walk out of the kitchen, where I stand guard most of the afternoon, I return to find someone drifting back into my pantry for more.

They are seed-harvester ants, and while me versus one boy is totally manageable, me versus the pack of them is nearly impossible. Their hunger is a lightsaber, and I am no match for its power.

Back in the days of more reasonably sized boxes, before I knew that a hundred-pack of granola bars even existed, I would get average servings of food that we would slowly eat up.

We started out just like regular people. I would buy the food, keep it on the shelf, and then give it to the boys when they asked. This was just before they realized they had super-powers and could scale walls and climb on ceilings. Back then, I didn't need to hide the food.

One day I caught my son Augie, six, getting into a box of snack cakes. I told him no, he needed to ask, and then moved the box higher. The next day, I caught another boy dangling off a pantry shelf, his fingers firmly planted into the highest rung. After the third incident, I realized this was a dangerous habit that was also terribly annoying. So I took drastic measures.

That night, after everyone had gone to bed, I shoved all the snacks into an empty box of bran flakes. Instead of putting the box high, I kept it down low, with all the other boring foods.

That worked for almost a week, before the boys either caught sight of me taking food out of the box or maybe just detected the glorious aroma of processed food seeping through the cardboard. Either way, the jig was up.

Slowly, as the years have progressed, we have left the world of mere mortal portions. We are now those people you see buying insane quantities that in theory will last me until the rapture but in reality will last until next week.

One day, I walked into the kitchen and told everyone to get out. They had eaten enough—snack time was over.

"You can't possibly need to eat anything else," I told them. "You're fine."

Out they scurried.

Ten minutes later, I walked back through to discover the lot of them starting up round two.

"Why are you still eating?" I asked in awe.

"Because"—someone munches—"we're still hungry."

Health Issues

The male species seems to have two settings for dealing with sickness: all or nothing. With my boys, it seems they are either in melodramatic agony or in denial. There is no in-between.

I shouldn't admit this, but it doesn't bother me when the boys are sick. I mean, it's not that I want them to get sick or that I enjoy watching them suffer. But there is something about those minor, non-life-threatening illnesses that force them to slow down long enough for me to catch hold of them and give them a good, long squeeze. I love those moments.

When my boys are nursing a fever or battling a stomach bug, they will lie on the couch and watch movies and let me kiss their forehead and rub their feet. Even my husband, an independent sort who is rarely sick, will tolerate my bringing his favorite drink and some chicken soup to him in bed.

Another positive aspect of the boys' being sick is that illness is generally the lone force strong enough to sideline a jousting match or suspend athletic competition.

But this only works when my boys admit they are sick or when the illness is severe enough to slow them down. The rest of the time we are at odds, me telling the boys (and my husband) that they need to go lie down, them telling me that they are really—*sniff, sniff*—totally—*cough, cough*—fine—*puke*.

One winter my husband had spent several weeks hobbling

along with a nasty cough. I asked him repeatedly to go see the doctor. He told me he was feeling better.

This went on too long, and finally Paul started feeling the effects. He came to me asking about medicine. I started to tell him about cough suppressants and decongestants, but before I could finish, he broke in.

"Do we have any Halls?" he asked. "I'd better take one of those."

I explained that cough drops were generally not considered medication that you would "take one of" and that, seeing as he had been battling this cough for over two weeks, he might want to try something stronger, like actual antibiotics. He said he'd think about it.

Not long after that, my oldest son, Ethan, twelve, got a nasty stomach bug. It was one of those violent tsunamis that came out of nowhere; it hit the poor child before he ever saw it coming.

One minute we were chatting with each other across the room; the next minute I looked up to see my son standing in a mess. I told him to go get in the shower and then he could lie on the couch.

Ten minutes later, that same boy came walking through the kitchen holding a stack of seven or eight chocolate chip cookies.

"Honey," I said after my initial shock, "that's too many."

He put one back.

"You may have two," I told him, recognizing the absurdity of a counteroffer.

"Three?" he asked, trying to bargain.

"Two," I asserted. "You just threw up all over my dining room floor."

"How about two and a half?"

Rations Irrational

One hot summer afternoon, Elliott, then eight, asked if he could make lunch for himself. Proud of his self-motivation and excited at the prospect of getting to sit still for an extra three minutes, I encouraged him to go right ahead.

Off he went while I sat and took note of a footprint on the ceiling and wondered how it got there. The problem with sitting still too long is that you discover a million little things you wish you hadn't. That's why it's so overrated.

Off in the kitchen I could hear the sounds of a boy at work—cabinets slamming, the fridge door opening and shutting. My son was humming to himself, no doubt delighted at the feast that would soon be his.

I started to wonder what he had opted to make—eggs with a side of fresh fruit? Perhaps turkey on wheat with sliced tomatoes accompanied by a crisp pickle. Maybe he was heating up the leftovers from last night's well-balanced dinner.

A few minutes later, I walked into the kitchen. There on the counter was his culinary masterpiece—a freshly nuked corn dog, surrounded by three kinds of chips. It was all laid out lovingly on a grease-stained paper towel.

Elliott was quite proud as he explained how he brought fruits and vegetables into his meal. There was corn in the tortillas, he pointed out, and tomatoes in the ketchup. And since corn dogs come from the most important food group, the one called *Awesome*, that just about covered it.

I stared at the array and marveled at his culinary prowess. I didn't know whether to celebrate his independence or check his cholesterol.

Sometimes I wonder if other mothers allow such meals. Would I be a better mother, I think, if I forced some shade of green onto this plate? Maybe I could grate zucchini on top of the Cheetos, or hide eggplant strips between the hot dog and the crispy corn coating. I bet he wouldn't notice an embedding of fresh tomato chunks in the ketchup.

But of course, I let him eat it as is.

There are those days when life feels like enough of a whirlwind without fixating on this one day with this one meal (and its abject lack of nutritional value). Some days I simply cannot stop long enough to nitpick about having enough purple or green or orange on the plate because I'm busy stopping the wrestling match in the front room or protecting my china cabinet from an errant soccer ball.

I also suspect that if I did raise that argument—the need for more "natural" color—Elliott would argue that the orange in these Doritos is all the orange he'll ever need.

I want to micromanage with daily charts and lists of what we should be eating, but I'm usually so caught up in making sure they don't literally gnaw the shelves off my pantry that I'm forced to relax on a few points.

We do the best we can. Some days are better than others, and I operate out of the truth that chewable vitamins were made with little boys in mind, and that I'll have another chance at perfection the *next* time this boy eats—about forty-five minutes from now.

The boys and I were taking a walk one afternoon. Baby Henry was in the stroller, Augie was on his scooter, Ethan walked next to me, while the last two rode their bikes.

At one point, the bikers were up ahead and I realized they had left the house without proper safety gear.

"I didn't make him wear a helmet," I said. "That's bad mothering."

"That's not bad mothering," said the boy walking next to me, "that's bad Scouting."

"I *am* like a Boy Scout," I marveled.

"You're a Girl Scout," said my son. "But they're not as cool—they only sell cookies. Do they even study birds or anything?"

"I can't remember," I told him.

"Well, Boy Scouts have fire," he noted with pride, and then ran off to catch up with his brothers.

Field Attire

I have a bad habit of making my boys dress alike. If you're not one of those people who find a need for "clothing congruity" obnoxious and sad, then you understand the appeal. I love the sense of satisfaction I get from seeing so many boys looking exactly the same, stair-step young lads bedecked in whatever I can find in their range of sizes.

Blame a lifetime of private-school uniforms, but I think buying five matching polo shirts just makes life easier.

I've certainly been on the receiving end of some serious ribbing for this yen. One Easter I sent out a picture of the boys looking dapper in matching spring-plaid oxfords. A friend told me they looked like the Osmond brothers. I took it as a compliment.

One afternoon we were watching ESPN and a commercial came on for *SportsCenter*, the show also known as Special Family Time Together. In the ad, three members of a popular basketball team walk through an office wearing their matching team jersey.

"Did you guys call each other?" an office worker asks, to which his co-worker adds, "Embarrassing!"

I started to laugh, and Elliott wanted to know what was so funny.

"It's funny that those guys are dressed alike."

"What's wrong with that?"

I explained that most people, women especially, don't want to show up somewhere wearing the same thing as someone else. "It's awkward," I told him.

"Then why," asked Ethan, "do you make us do it all the time?"

A huge pull in my dressing the boys, of course, is that it controls what they are wearing. I'm all for freedom of expression, but the way my boys choose to "express" themselves is, style-wise, terribly unstylish. One of the most challenging aspects of a household of boys is the issue of clothes. The males in this household have clothing preferences that are sometimes a cause for concern.

One morning when Augie was four, he had Field Day at his preschool. Children were encouraged to wear red, white, and blue. Easy enough, I thought. I surveyed my son's wardrobe and honed in on a crisp red T-shirt and newish blue soccer shorts.

But the morning of school, he came downstairs wearing a two-sizes-too-small Atlanta Braves T-shirt and some worn-out shorts. The oversized shorts hung well below his knees, while the T-shirt did not even cover his belly button.

My thoughts went to the sweet little girls who would be wearing their finest smocked dresses, and I cried in my corn flakes. While I no longer aspire for Little Lord Fauntleroy, is an anatomically proportionate outfit too much to ask?

Striking a balance in the clothing issue is tough, mostly because I've found the boys do not inherently care about style. Perhaps they will as they get older, but right now, their idea of looking "nice" is wearing a T-shirt with less than five stains on the front.

Elliott likes to wear the same basketball jersey every single day as he shoots hoops in the driveway. If we have to go to the store and I ask him to put on something suitable for the viewing public, he throws on a white Hanes T-shirt underneath the tank top he's already wearing.

One evening Paul and I took the boys to a wake. When it was time to get dressed, I explained to the boys what a wake was and that we go to honor the person who has died. Then I sent them upstairs to find appropriate clothes.

A few minutes later, Augie came back down. He wore a ragged-out T-shirt inherited from a brother, paired with gray basketball shorts in a polyester sheen. On his head was a sweatband so grimy that it seemed to coordinate with his shorts, though the band was in fact originally white.

"Absolutely not," I said, steadying my face from any hint of surprise.

"Dang it," was his reply. He honestly thought I would approve.

I suspect he does this to make me appreciate the beauty of a clean golf shirt. When the boys were very little, they did wear coveralls. I figured this would go on forever (don't they make them in a 12 slim?), and now realize that I'm happy if they're all wearing shoes.

Wouldn't it be great, I once romanticized, if on the day of the school Easter party, my boys wanted to wear golf shirts in festive spring colors, instead of camouflage pants and a striped turtleneck?

Do the clothes make the man? It's hard to say. My husband is a very good dresser, but he also has a tendency to wear clothes he's had since law school. When he's not wearing suits and ties to meet with clients at the office, he opts for the same oversized athletic shorts and a T-shirt from his first 5K years ago. And I wonder where my boys get it.

Sometimes, I think, I give them all too much credit. I

assume they are choosing clothes because of comfort or aesthetics. For years, I put up with my husband's favorite shirt because I thought it held sentimental value. I finally decided to broach the subject.

"What do you like so much about this?" I gently asked, holding up the bulky red Henley with blue sleeves.

"I'm not sure," he said.

"I think," I ventured, "it's because your mother gave it to you."

"She did?"

"Yes," I said. "It's one of the last gifts she gave you before she died."

"It is?"

And that was the last we saw of ol' blue (and red). The shirt held none of the suspected emotional attachment, and thus there was no reason to keep it.

I know I should feel relieved, that opting for ragged basketball clothes is so much better than the alternative. Once, after we saw a movie about Mexican wrestling, my boys spent several days walking around with underwear on the outside of their pants and also over their faces. I was able to convince them, without too much effort, that underwear on your face in public crosses a line that we shouldn't be anywhere near.

The boys are beginning to understand that I have standards, standards that seem to get lower by the minute. They have accepted that certain occasions will warrant a certain kind of dress, and that some of these events will almost always involve the lot of them looking alike.

"Mom," said nine-year-old Charlie one spring, "do we all have to dress the same this Easter?"

"What do you think?" I asked. I wondered if he was on to my wicked ways.

"Yes," he said in a resigned tone.

And he's right. For as long as I can make it happen, I will dress the boys alike. I know it won't last forever—at least, I don't think it will. But you never know. Maybe they'll think it's just part of being on a team.

Objects of Affection

One of the sweetest moments of my day is checking the pockets of my boys' clothes as I load the washing machine. On the windowsill in the laundry room, I line up whatever items I find until I run out of room, purge, and start the process again.

Items range from the obvious to the surprising. Typical finds include rocks, batteries, LEGOS, and shards of glass. There are bottle caps, chips of wood, tiny pencils, and dice. I find leaves on a regular basis and shark teeth occasionally.

While the majority of items come and go, I keep on the windowsill three items that have stood the test of time— items that I love because they indicate the sharp eye and good taste each of my boys possess.

The first item is an old wooden spool, an antique that I can't imagine where they found. I love that whichever boy found this spool recognized its vintage charm.

The next item is a piece of rock, a white granite shard shaped like a five-point star. I was walking through a parking lot one evening at dusk when my boy spotted this. I still remember the awe I felt when my five-year-old bent down to grab the rock, honing in on this one in a sea of so many.

"Look what my son spotted!" I wanted to shout. "Did anyone else notice this rock shaped like a star?" But I did not shout, which I imagine was a brilliant move on my part.

The third item is a tiny green plastic ninja, about the size of a six-year-old's pinky. We have at least a dozen tiny plastic ninjas floating around our house. I like what this says about my life.

My boys don't always come home from school ready to dish about the day. But if I'm patient, little details will reveal themselves to me. When I check the pockets, I get a peek into my boys' minds, an idea of what they consider amazing and lovely—what they consider to be a thing of beauty.

I feel lucky to get a glimpse of this beauty every day.

Proper Care and Feeding

The Spies Who Loved Me

One Saturday afternoon on a family clothes shopping trip, the boys were at the end of an apparel aisle while Paul and I were preoccupied with a search for boys' sports coats. Every few minutes I'd look up to make sure they were still a few feet away, and each time I looked, they were engrossed in winter hats.

"Look what we found," said a voice a few minutes later, and I turned to discover a sea of heads covered in ski masks, a pint-sized SWAT team standing at our elbows. I wasn't sure who was who, or even if these were in fact my children. Perhaps I was about to be robbed by a group of pygmies disguised as athletic urchins.

"Wow," I finally mustered, "where did you find those?"

"Aren't they awesome?" said one muffled voice, the boy's mouth partially covered by his misaligned mask. "Can we get them?"

My thoughts turned to our daily mile-long trek to school. When the cold weather hits, I told myself, they will want to wear these on that walk—what if someone mistakes us for a set of prep-school bank robbers, led by a stroller-pushing crazy woman?

"I don't know," I stalled, "those look pretty itchy."

"They're not itchy," said another boy, "they're AWE-SOME."

The boys wandered back to the hat rack while Paul and I finished our search for the perfect sports coat, one sturdy enough to last through four other boys, but one that the oldest boy would not outgrow immediately.

After staying in the coats section slightly longer than we should have, it was time to move on. I wondered if the boys had lost interest in the hats, if we could leave the store without them. I turned to call the boys and discovered the lot of them still bedecked in woolen head garb.

There was something sweet and hilarious about the pack of them wanting these hats so badly. I knew we could tell them no, but instead, I told them to make their selections and bring them along.

For days after that, the boys wore the hats whenever they could. Despite the 80-plus temps, I would look in the backyard to find our four older boys wrestling or racing or even playing soccer—all while wearing black and blue ski masks.

On the way to church that Sunday, the radio was on and everyone was quiet. The windows were all rolled down, and I looked in the rearview mirror to discover all the boys staring out. Three of them were wearing ski masks.

A minute later, we pulled up next to a fire engine. I turned to look just as the men in the truck noticed my boys. I saw them laugh. Our car shot ahead, but a minute later, the fire truck pulled up next to us. In the back of the truck, one fireman sported the specially fabricated hat that goes under the fire helmet—he had donned his own ski mask to match the boys.

We all laughed—me and Paul, the boys, and the truckload of firefighters. We smiled and waved until we pulled ahead and out of sight.

"That," said eight-year-old Charlie, "was just too good."

We are getting ready to leave the house. "Something is wrong with your hair," says ten-year-old Elliott. I reach up to feel the hot rollers I threw in a few minutes earlier.

"Are you going out like that?" he asks.

I look at this boy: he is wearing a cotton shirt that is gray and blue, and a pair of shorts that are gray and white. Like the shirt, these shorts are striped, but in a different direction and color. They are the same shorts he has worn nearly every day of Christmas break. The other night I had to wrestle them off his body, and was only successful because he was physically ill.

"These aren't dirty," he said, walking into the laundry room to find them in the hamper. "They're perfectly clean."

"Son," I answered, "you just threw up while wearing them."

"Okay," he surrendered, "but I want to wear them tomorrow."

This is the child who is questioning my looks before we leave the house.

Sigh.

Hygienically Challenged

One of my most lofty goals as the mother of boys is to have my sons aware of and striving for personal hygiene before they leave for college. I think this is realistic—mothers all over the world very nearly pull this off all the time.

But I might have to settle for this as my life opus. At this stage of the game, with everyone in middle school and younger, it seems like their ability to have clean teeth and feet and armpits rests solely on my shoulders. When I fall down on the job, we all suffer.

When our fifth son, Henry, was born, the four older boys went next door to stay with my parents. Each boy packed a bag before I left for the hospital, and I checked to make sure it included pajamas and toothbrushes and the necessary number of underpants—the count by my standards, of course, not the boys'. My sons stayed with Gramma and Papa for one or two nights, then packed up their bags and came home.

Several days later, when Henry was about a week old, one of my brothers came to visit after being next door. "Here," he said, holding four toothbrushes, "these were at Mom and Dad's."

For almost an entire week, the boys went without brushing their teeth. And no one noticed, not even me. I felt a bit sick to my stomach. I am a terrible mother, I realized, and my children have terrible breath.

I quickly got over my pity party, opting instead to channel that energy toward conquering halitosis and body odor. That episode was really just a friendly reminder that I've got my work cut out for me—I will make my boys hygienic, despite their efforts to thwart me. And while I'm at it, I will learn that the best way to determine the cleanliness of a pair of underwear is not to burrow my nose in them. That almost never ends well.

Around here, dirty clothes can be toxic. When Ethan was in fifth grade, his class took its first field trip involving long travel and change of clothes. The group left before school started and got home that evening just before bedtime. The day was long and wonderful, and absolutely met my son's breathless anticipation.

That evening my tired but happy boy came home just as his brothers were finishing bath time. I told my son he needed to hop in the shower—he had hiked through the woods, gone swimming in the ocean, and traveled several hours each way in a van filled with other sweaty fifth-grade boys.

"But, Mom," he pleaded, "I practically showered already."

"What does that mean?" I asked.

"I washed my face like four times today!"

"Wanna get some free food, Mama?" asks eight-year-old Charlie, looking up from his book on predatory wildlife.

"Sure," I tell him.

"Okay," he says, "first, you're gonna need a cheetah."

Hair

One morning I was helping our first grader do some finishing touches on his appearance before leaving for school. I reached for the dollar-store spray bottle we use to tame unwieldy bed head and started to wet his hair.

"It's cold," he complained. "Why do you always fill it with cold water?"

"I don't refill it every morning," I explained before trying to calculate how long it had been since we'd freshened up the water. Could I even remember?

"Does the barber use warm water?" I asked.

While waiting for an answer, I started to think about the basic approach to haircuts we get at the barbershop.

When we enter the building, things move like clockwork: in chair, plastic cape around neck, spray, cut, and done. I sit with the other boys while they wait, and we take turns reading whatever manly magazines are available.

One week, as nine-year-old Elliott waited his turn, he settled on a copy of *Hunting* magazine to pass the time.

"*Guns and Ammo* is better than this," he said, flipping the pages. He read quietly for a minute and then turned to me. "I was *on fire* today in math. You wouldn't believe."

The barbershop brings out the man in my boys. Something tells me in a place like that, the spray bottle water isn't freshened every day.

Then I started thinking about my own experience when getting a haircut. When I go for a cut and color, I am ushered into the salon with relaxing music and forgiving lights. I'm led back to the sink, gently reclined, and given a five-minute scalp massage before having a thorough wash with herbal-infused shampoo and conditioner. Then it's on to a precision haircut followed by a precision blow-dry, all while surrounded by oil paintings and the latest copies of *Architectural Digest*.

I look down at the cheapo spray bottle in my hand and head for the sink. Suddenly my son's request that I fill it with warm water didn't seem like too much to ask.

Hygiene Wars

One evening, the night before the boys' school pictures, I was panicked. Too long had I taken a laissez-faire approach to their dental hygiene. I needed to force each of my sons to brush his teeth. I finally admitted to myself that this is what hygiene is going to take around here—me physically dragging boys into the bathroom and brushing their teeth myself.

That I can admit this here shows how much I've grown in recent history. There was a time—a long, long time—that I saw my boys' approach to hygiene as a direct reflection of how I was doing as a mother. You don't want to brush your teeth? I'm a failure.

One day I finally asked my husband what I was up against.

"Why don't our sons care about how they smell?" I asked.

"They're young," was his reply, telling me he didn't start really brushing until high school. How I never knew this I cannot be sure. Again, another detail of my life that would have been nice to know beforehand. Boys don't take it upon themselves to smell fresh and crisp. Then again, why does this surprise me?

As I dragged each of my boys into the bathroom that evening, I forced them to stand still. With each one of these boys, from the first grader all the way up to my middle school student, I lathered and chipped and scrubbed each tooth.

"We're playing dentist," I cheered. "Isn't this great!"

They couldn't answer, which was a very good thing.

At one point, as I held Ethan in my clutches, I got greedy. I eyed his teeth and decided I would not only brush them— I'd floss them as well!

I took out the dental pick and started to work my magic. In and out went the floss, moving amongst the teeth. What I discovered made me weep, a thrilling mixture of awe and glee with a hint of nausea.

A minute later, I hauled in Elliott and did the same. After a while, so high from my success, I wanted it all.

"And now," I told them, "we're going to have a gargling contest."

Their ears perked up. Contest? Yes, now we're talking.

I gave each boy a swig of mouthwash and told them we'd see who could swish the longest, myself included.

We threw back our heads and started to swirl. After nearly a minute, I leaned over the sink and dispensed of my load. The boys kept going—ten seconds, twenty—and I knew we were approaching the target time of two minutes.

Soon after, the boys threw in the towel and spit out the wash.

"Smell my breath," said Charlie. And I did so with delight.

"Isn't that better?" I asked. "Now do you see why you need to brush?"

"I'm going to start doing this all the time," said my oldest, "maybe even once a month."

HairDo's (and Don'ts)

The boys have been on a kick about hair, and as two of their favorite things on earth are competition and winning, having a competition about who can have the best hairdo seems like a logical next step.

One evening I walk into my bathroom to overhear a conversation. On this particular evening, the boys are discussing a hairdo contest that involves racing to see who can get the best coif the fastest. I listen as the rules and guidelines are explained—a rundown of how to play and, more importantly, how to win.

Each round, announces the leader, will have someone who names an occasion. Each player will then have only a few seconds to style the coif that best fits that occasion. The round leader will then choose a winner.

As I stand and eavesdrop, I am intrigued. The boys fight me tooth and nail every Sunday when it's time to leave for church—they practically run in the opposite direction when they see me coming toward them with a comb. One boy's idea of dressing up is promising to wear the pants with the nice knee patches.

I am in awe of this game on so many levels. I marvel not just that they want to do their hair, but that they know how to do it. I am probably most astounded that they realize more than one hairstyle exists.

The rules are explained and it's time for round one.

"This is the . . . wedding round!" the leader shouts. "Go!"

It's obvious we've been to a few weddings recently—four family weddings this year—and they are indeed professionals at how to look and act at such an occasion. Several seconds go by before the three players examine their handiwork in the mirror across the bathroom. Each boy has his hair slicked perfectly—one boy straight back, two with stark parts running down the scalp.

A winner is chosen, the boy whose bangs are plastered to his forehead, and it's on to round two.

This goes on for a while, with rounds for church or ball games or just hanging around. Round after round, an occasion is announced and the styling ensues.

Eventually, someone cries foul. I go back in to check on things and discover a disgruntled, very nicely coifed boy who is standing in my bathroom.

The latest round, he explains, was left blank—a free-for-all with judging based on hairstyle alone. The boy with the nice hairdo lost to the boy with the Mohawk, and I find myself pleased and comforted that some things never change.

An Uphill Battle

One summer afternoon, as I walk from one side of the house to the other, I find myself saying the same thing over and over and over again.

"Boys," I call as I enter the laundry room, "where is the—who did this?"

There are melted popsicles on the laundry table, beach towels in a pile on the floor. A picture has been knocked off the wall and rests where it landed near the baseboard.

I get to the bottom of that mess, and head toward the front door.

"I'm going to get the mail—who did *this*?"

A discarded popsicle wrapper sticks to the coffee table in the front room.

I deal with that, check the mailbox, and come back in.

"Yes, you may watch a show," I answer, and just then I pass the recently wiped-down bathroom to find someone's aim was not true. "WHO DID THIS?"

I sound like someone on a game show trying to be the first to say the winning phrase. But I don't feel like I'm winning.

It would be naïve of me to hope for too much. I don't expect the boys to yearn for the opportunity to wipe down surfaces with warm, soapy water. They are not their mother, after all. But some days we are a little too far off of a happy medium.

I'm feeling hopeful, though. I recently discovered that boys really will work for food. The daunting task of getting them to make their beds has become a non-issue simply by dangling a little fruit-flavored carrot in front of their noses.

"Whoever makes their bed gets an extra snack in their lunch," I say, and the sound of feet scampering upstairs completes that thought.

Like mothers everywhere, I'm training my children to get the job done. I'm happy to report that our path to motivation seems straight and narrow—right down the center of my grocer's snack aisle.

Let Your Aim Be True

One thing I have discovered about moms of boys—we can talk about the toilet for an awfully long time. For someone who once gave no thought to the mechanics of getting body fluid from Point A to Point B, I am amazed at what an expert I have become.

I know, for instance, that the best way to get your sons to pee directly into the toilet is to have a target floating in the latrine. It might be a Cheerio or a chunk of debris, but if something is in the bowl, a boy will be helpless to resist.

My six-year-old exited the bathroom in utter mirth one afternoon.

"Mom," he said, laughing, "I just peed on a leaf that was floating in the pot."

Little did he know I had put that leaf there for the very purpose of target practice. That leaf not only drew my son's attention, but it saved me from having to wipe down the floor for at least another thirty minutes.

I am continually amazed that an inherent love of sports doesn't carry over into a boy's bathroom etiquette.

"You would never be happy totally missing the basket when you shoot hoops," I explain as I go over the rules of bathroom use. (Step 1: aim for the toilet. Step 2: aim away from the floor.)

In addition to target practice, moms of boys have likely

researched the best type of toilet seat and what product is most effective for getting rid of a relentless urine odor in the bathroom. We know these things because of trial and error—or we are desperate to know and we want to hear from the experts.

When it's all said and done, I'm guessing we'll be experts in countless fields that we never could have imagined.

"Mom," Elliott declares, pulling his nose out of his shoes after inhaling deeply, "my tennis shoes don't smell like rotten fish anymore."

SHOPPING:
THE SEVEN RINGS OF SUFFERING

1. Shopping for sports equipment—this is the least painful of all the shopping excursions, made easier by the fact that shopping will result in cool stuff for those who shop with a good attitude. Also, you get to play on sports equipment while parents make purchases. Highlight of this trip includes two boys getting on the elliptical trainer, one boy per pedal, and whipping themselves into a frenzy.

2. Shopping for food—this next ring involves buying stuff to eat and drink, which is always a good thing. Slightly more painful than sports shopping, because this also involves buying vegetables and fruit which, while not too bad to eat, takes away from time looking at two-liter bottles of Dr Pepper and begging Mom for Cocoa Puffs and lunchables.

3. Shopping for toys—yes, it's odd that this one would be on a list of suffering. This is a sad side effect of having to hear the word "no" more than one would like. This makes the trip far less enjoyable. Also, the boys have figured out that Mom is more inclined to say yes to requests for sports equipment, and not toys, because these requests involve being outside, which is something we're all for around here. Shopping for toys, on the other hand, usually involves Mom trying not to roll her eyes at all the useless pieces of plastic that are available for purchase.

4. Shopping for tools—at some point in their life, this kind of shopping excursion will move to the top of the list as the shopping trip that is Least Undesirable (not to be confused with Most Desirable, which is a concept that does not include shopping). For Dad, going to the hardware store brings him the greatest satisfaction of all the shopping sufferings, but would still never be desirable over, say, hitting golf balls in the backyard or even polishing shoes while watching a football game.

5. Shopping for clothes—the less said on this subject, the better. Mom still gets a nervous tic at the thought of these excursions.

6. Shopping for nothing, also known as window-shopping—this is the ultimate in shopping torture, because there is no end in sight, no list to mark off that ensures we will reach our goal and get to leave the store. However, it still doesn't top the list, because even with shopping for nothing, there is always the possibility that in the midst of the endless, mind-numbing wandering, one will come across something, a ball perhaps, that will momentarily take one's mind off the pain of walking aisle after aisle.

7. Shopping for furniture—the worst kind of suffering. What is the point of getting new stuff when Mom is just going to tell us we can't jump off it or do front flips on it or eat in its vicinity? Really, getting new furniture is more like torture, and having to walk slowly and quietly through a store full of it is only slightly more painful.

2

. . . .

You Know You're
with Boys
When . . .

Competition

When the boys were very little, I could often get them to move faster with a challenge. If it was time for bed, instead of turning our nighttime rituals into a battle, I would simply ask who could be the quickest to get on his pajamas. It was a beautiful sight at the end of those very long days. Off they would go—four tiny little bodies scampering to be the first one ready for bed.

When I initially discovered this jewel called competition, I could not believe my good fortune.

Thinking back to the season when our oldest four were all so little, I'm pretty sure I was the one motivating these challenges. While I wholeheartedly believe boys are hardwired for competition, our early days of competition were fully for my benefit and usually born of my quick thinking.

In the morning, I would ask who could be the first boy to get dressed for the day. Before naptime, we would see how fast we could pick up the playroom. When leaving to run errands, it was a race to see how fast we could climb into the car and get in our car seats!

This was my secret weapon, made more beautiful by the fact that the boys did not catch on. My sons didn't realize they were making my life exponentially easier—they just wanted to be fast.

At some point, however, we crossed a threshold. Our

challenges started as quarter-mile Tot Trots and have morphed into the 10Ks of today. Around here, there is no task unworthy of competition, no feat too big or small, when it comes to trying to dominate a brother with acts of speed and agility.

One day when I was emptying the dishwasher, I noticed a piece of Scotch tape on one of my Mexican juice glasses. I scraped off the tape and put away the glass. I pulled out another glass from the dishwasher and noticed it too had a piece of tape. As I worked to clean the second glass, I tried to figure out what the tape meant. As it made no sense to me, however, I simply put away the glass and forgot all about it.

Later that day, I found my oldest two boys in the dining room. On the table were two glasses marked with tape, like those I found earlier. One boy was pouring milk into each glass

"What's going on?" I asked.

"We're having a race," he said as he carefully decanted, "to see who can drink milk the fastest."

"Why the tape?" I asked the other boy.

"To make sure we have the exact same amount."

When the milk was poured, each boy held up his glass to the other. The levels were acceptable, and the chugging began.

Being a girl, I do have limits. I made it very clear early on that we will not compete when it comes to food. There are no eating contests—while my boys don't want to draw the line at danger, I certainly do.

We dove headfirst into this era of competition, and I don't foresee us outgrowing it. Ever. The range of what boys will compete over is vast and impressive. Based on what I have seen from other households of boys, the Family Balducci is only just scratching the surface.

When my husband was in college, he and his roommates

would spend hours in heated discussions about various competitions. Even talking about competition became a competition.

He and his buddies would argue about which professional player was the most athletic, who was the strongest and fastest and best. They would try to hash out who would win between Player A and Player B, or Team C versus Team D. Sometimes they'd do Player E against Team F and then include a wide range of other variables as well.

They would fight about Larry Byrd versus Magic Johnson, or who would win in a contest between Herschel Walker and the entire Notre Dame defense.

"Many discussions," my husband explained one afternoon, "revolved around Chuck Norris, and what he would do in a given situation."

You can see exactly where all this is headed.

Currently in our home, competitions range from the obvious (who can make the most free throws) to the slightly trickier (who can catch the most popcorn kernels on his tongue in a row). There is walking in the door first, calling shotgun first, and being the first person to jump in the pool during summer swim league. I even use their competitive nature for musical gains, challenging the boys to see who can practice his instrument more consistently and with greater return.

While there are those times when competition makes things go faster, what I'm waiting for is a direct impact on my standard of living. I wonder when they'll duke it out over quickest to mop the entire downstairs or first to fall asleep. Will I get this lucky?

Also, because I'm a girl, I work hard to keep all this competition within reason. This is getting harder as the boys get older. There's nothing like a little friendly competition, but some days the challenge is keeping it little (and friendly).

(Little) Boys Behaving Badly

Historically, we as a family have always done marginally well buying food together, a camaraderie due in large part to a sense of "I'd better pay attention because that's what I'll be forced to eat later on."

Sometimes, however, I go through tough seasons. Life is filled with scheduling conflicts and imbalances in the universe. Sometimes out of desperation, I do the unthinkable.

I take the boys shopping with me—to someplace other than the grocery store.

One year on Earth Day, we bought a tree to plant in our front yard. My husband needed a few new tools to make the experience a pleasant one, and off we went to the one store where a man doesn't demand an end time to the trip. Will it take minutes? Hours? Days? Whatever! It's all good!

We got to the home improvement store, and since Paul was instantly drunk on the splendor that is a tools and hardware section the size of a small country, I took over keeping all the boys in one continent of the store.

At some point, one boy noticed there were birds that live in the rafters of the indoor gardening section, and it was then that Paul called me over to look at the shovels he'd picked out. In the instant it took for me to turn my glance from my boys to my husband, seven-year-old Charlie grabbed something from a lower hook and took off running.

By the time I raced to the end of the aisle and got him in my sights, the boy was several hundred feet ahead, sprinting after his brother. He was running full speed, laughing wildly while wielding a pitchfork.

"Charlie!" I yelled, in awe of his behavior.

"He's a bad guy," he hollered over his shoulder. "I'm chasing him."

We headed for the car soon after that.

I guess I didn't learn my lesson. Several days later, I was forced to take Augie and Charlie to the local Latin foods shop to get supplies for a Cinco de Mayo party. They seemed to be in a well enough place mentally, but I had my reservations. We were on the way home from school, before snacks, before naps, and I can never be sure why this seemed like a good idea.

Upon entering the shop, the two boys loosed themselves from me and started to wander. It was all harmless enough initially. We were the only shoppers, and I could hear everything they said and did as they surveyed the scene.

After a few minutes, the boys started getting slightly rambunctious, and I pulled them over with me. But a split second later, as I perused cans of mango and guava juice, I heard a scream from the tiny woman behind the counter.

"Aiiii! Aiiii-yaiiii-yaaaiiiii!"

I looked around the corner to find my three-year-old standing in a pint-sized refrigerator, his five-year-old brother trying to close the door.

"Es danger!" she shouted. And of course it was.

I grabbed my son by the arm and yanked the too-willing victim from the fridge. Fighting back tears, I headed for the door.

"Oh, es so daaaangerous," I heard the woman telling a customer who had since come in.

"It *is* dangerous," I said, distancing myself from the antics. As if I too were merely a horrified bystander in awe of the logic-defying acts of these tiny humans.

The problem in this situation was that this was not a teachable moment—a chance to learn about a new and dangerous behavior we should avoid. The problem was, this was a moment we had already covered.

In our home, we actually have a rule about not shutting people in the fridge. Because it is dangerous, and because it had already been tried before. In addition to not shutting your brother in the kitchen refrigerator, the boys have been schooled in the importance of staying away from any abandoned appliance, in the unlikely event that they would come across one.

So on that day, in that little shop, not only was I embarrassed, but I also had to deal with the ramifications of the boys breaking an actual rule that I am forced to have in my home: Don't shut your brother in an oversized appliance.

As I stewed in my frustration and fought off self-pity, I considered the possibility that the male species might just do whatever it takes to cut a shopping trip short.

Personality

Despite being the same gender from the same father and mother, my boys each approach life in a totally different way. While this fact can be quite frustrating at times (my husband and I have a different plan of action for each boy for each behavior), I am also quite intrigued. How surprising it always is to see how their personalities affect their approach to life, to dilemmas and conflict and just relating to others in general.

I am particularly intrigued by my oldest son, Ethan, because he has a way of handling requests and hopes and dreams that is either totally different from me or exactly like me; I can't decide. I am especially in awe of his diplomacy and legal finesse—in those areas, he takes after his father.

One afternoon I took the boys out to lunch. As all the other schools in the area were already back in session, we had the play place of the restaurant to ourselves.

I was sitting with Henry, feeding him bits of food, while the older boys enjoyed sliding and crawling and climbing all over the indoor playground. I wasn't paying much attention to their behavior because everyone was getting along, no one was getting hurt, and (most importantly) we were the only family in the area and thus guaranteed not to bother anyone.

At one point Elliott walked over to me, a little sweaty from all the exercise.

"It will be awesome," he said with a smile, "if we don't get caught."

"Get caught," I asked, alarmed, "doing what?"

"The sign says no climbing," Elliott said.

"It says no *climbing*," said Ethan, walking over to us, "but we aren't climbing. We're monkeying around."

Latest Issue
from the House of Tissue

I kept everyone home from school one day, a preemptive strike as much as anything else. Ethan seemed bona fide "puny," but the other boys could have gone either way. I was hoping for a day of laying low, watching some movies, and getting caught up on rest. This way we could avoid getting totally worn down and officially out of commission.

Unfortunately, boys who are not actually sick but are kept home to act like they are sick will not act like they are sick. They won't embrace the whole "we're sick, let's hunker down and recover" vibe, no matter how hard you send it. I learned a valuable lesson that day.

That afternoon I went out to the car for two seconds. When I came back into the house and entered the front room, I found Charlie at the very top of the staircase, holding on to the railings on the *outside*.

"Are you guys ready for my BELLY FLOP?" he yelled. I commanded him to stop. I don't care if there is a pile of pillows on the floor. You are going to get hurt. Trust me.

It turned into a day of the one truly sick boy mindlessly staring off into space in a fever-induced haze while his healthy brothers lived *la vida loca* all around him.

"How do you spell *leech*?" Elliott had asked earlier in the day. He was in the midst of an early-morning drawing craze.

Who draws leeches at eight in the morning? I marveled, before realizing the bittersweet answer: We do.

On that day of infirmity, I watched as my boys built LEGO rocket ships; drew with crayons, then with markers, then with colored pencils; draped themselves in leopard-print fur; and tied up each other with shiny gold cord. There was a little wailing, some tears, and the requisite minimal fighting. Mostly, though, it was a day of good old-fashioned brotherly fun—for the healthy ones anyway.

"Let's play Army," said Augie, deciding it was time for a new activity.

"I'm sick," rasped Ethan.

"Me too," said Charlie as he gathered camouflage for the next round of fun. But he wasn't sick at all, and he did a very poor job of acting the part.

"Let's have a math contest," one boy tells his brothers. "You have to answer the math problem before this timer rings, and if you get it wrong . . . I punch you in the kidneys."

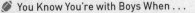 You Know You're with Boys When . . .

Making Plans

Eight-year-old Charlie has a playdate on his calendar. He comes home from school the day before with a note from his friend.

"Things to do," writes the friend, who proceeds to list all the amazing and fun activities the two boys will be enjoying:

1. play Legos
2. play Lego Star Wars the Game
3. play outside

The list goes up to number nine and includes things like "play soccer" and "hunt for slugs." There is also a side note about the need for Charlie to just tell the hosting friend if he gets hungry.

In the meantime, six-year-old Augie is making plans for his upcoming birthday party.

"Why don't you write down exactly who you'd like to invite," I tell him, "and also what you want to do?"

A few minutes later, he brings me a slip of paper. On it are the names of his dearest friends and cousins, and the list of activities he wants the party to include:

waterslide
water balloon
fite

Another perfect get-together waiting to happen.

Dangerous Living

My definition of living on the edge: leaving a Sharpie within reach of the boys.

One Christmas our home was in full-throttle Beatlemania. Paul had recently purchased *Yellow Submarine*, and the boys were watching this psychedelic gem of a flick every chance they got.

I was doing a project using my black permanent marker one afternoon. At some point, in the middle of my craft, one of the boys called for help, and I walked away from my workstation to see what he needed.

When I came back a few minutes later, my marker was gone.

Meanwhile, Ethan, then nine years old, also went missing. I didn't think much of it and instead focused my efforts on the missing marker.

A few minutes later, my son emerged. He walked out of a nearby room wearing a wool cap and sporting stylized black marker all over his face. He had given himself overgrown eyebrows, a mustache, and long sideburns straight from the era of peace and love. He looked just like his favorite cartoon Beatle in his new favorite cartoon Beatle movie.

"Wha . . . who . . . *arghhh*!" That was all I could get out in between heavy, labored breaths.

We were scheduled to take Christmas card photos the

next day, and in that moment, as I processed the sight of Ethan standing before me, I imagined hundreds of my closest friends, relatives, and former classmates opening a card from Our Family. They would be greeted by the lovely image of our four boys: Elliott, Charlie, Augie, and Paul McCartney as a cartoon character?

I willed myself not to hyperventilate as I grabbed a washcloth and started to scrub. Furiously I lathered, mentally preparing myself for the reality of a nine-year-old with tattooed facial hair.

I began to rinse, and to my utter amazement the ink came off. The more I rinsed, the cleaner became my son's face. So unexpected was this result, so not the nature of permanent black markers.

When I asked for the pen, Ethan produced a washable marker. He had grabbed one of the markers they always use, the ones I keep in the art box, the kind I don't keep in the family safe.

Later on, I found my Sharpie above the microwave, where I always keep it. I had been spared having a cartoon character for a son—I was delighted by this simple bit of luck.

Danger and
All of Her Accessories

We drive by a construction site, a patch off the highway that is a work in progress. In the large area is a crane, a jackhammer, a remote control flattener, and some sort of front digger.

"I love construction work," sighs Charlie, looking out the window. "I love everything about it—the machines, the work, everything."

"When I grow up," says Augie, "I want to be one of those workers."

We wait at the nearby stoplight and they continue to watch.

"Imagine being under one of those," says Charlie, watching the machine that is flattening the earth.

"That," says Ethan, "or being in it."

My sons, they would take it either way.

After all these years with boys, I am still amazed at how boyish they really are. All the stereotypes you hear about boys are true—they love trucks and weapons and running with knives. They want to hang off the side of a moving vehicle, and build things and take things apart. They love danger and all of her accessories.

I once caught Charlie on the top of our playground slide, hunched over with a long stick in each hand. He was about to ski down the plastic yellow slope before I stopped him, sadly just as he was readying for takeoff. He was genuinely confused as to why I would squelch his efforts.

When they grow up, boys want to be all those things you would guess—a construction worker or a fireman or possibly a superhero, depending on what powers that would involve. They want those things for you too.

One of the boys once told me he thought it would be cool if I could add a few more titles to my job description.

"What if you were a mother slash assassin slash double agent?" he asked, gazing into my eyes as if it were already so.

But there is this other side, a side that includes gentility and tenderness and, if you're lucky, a little bit of culture. There are those moments when, instead of trying to find out how many words rhyme with *toot*, a boy will ask you the definition of the word *classic* or *contrast* or for an example of iambic pentameter.

One afternoon I overheard the tail end of an argument between two of the boys.

"Why are you so obsessed with Beethoven?" asked Charlie, fed up with his brother. It seems there is a limit to how many times a person can listen to *Für Elise* being tickled on the ivories.

A few days later, Augie was roaming through the house in search of food.

"I'm starving," he declared loudly, "and I don't want edamame."

These moments give me a glimpse into the other side of boys, the side that goes beyond what I have come to expect. It is sweet and funny, and on the harshest of days, it is just enough to keep me going.

Call Waiting

My children have a phone allergy. It's genetic—they get it from their father.

A friend called one day, and my oldest son answered the phone.

"In all my years of calling you," said she, who has known me since we were eight, "that is maybe the second time one of your boys has answered the phone."

A telephone to my boys is what a piranha is to me—a strange, curious-looking creature that is dangerous to the touch. The phone will ring, and if I am in another part of the house or unable to answer, I will have to beg and plead for someone, anyone, to pick up.

"Does anyone hear that ringing sound?" I'll holler. "Someone walk toward that noise and there will be a black rectangle with some sound coming out of it."

"I found it!" someone will yell back.

"Good," I'll say. "Now push the green button, the one that says 'talk.'"

"Got it!"

"Now talk!"

Few are the times they follow through on that last directive. In the rare instance I convince them to pick up the phone ("It won't bite, I promise!"), they will answer the phone by simply turning it on. Then they'll walk through the house

65

calling my name, searching for me to take this heavy burden from them.

By the time I get the phone, the caller has been treated to the sounds of a stampede of young male humans traveling through the house. They are a pack of young cubs in search of their fearless leader. Only she has the power to use this mystical, mysterious device.

I would say they are bound to outgrow this, but I'm not hopeful. My husband does the same thing.

"It's for you," he'll say, looking at the caller ID before pushing TALK, handing me the phone, and running in the opposite direction.

Questionably Self-Sufficient

Not long ago, when we had a babysitter over for the afternoon, a misunderstanding broke out. The boys perceived her behavior as being rude and threatening. They claimed she treated the baby in a less-than-acceptable fashion.

"Henry got hurt," Elliott told me later, "and when he started to cry, she just rolled her eyes."

So the boys grouped up into a huddle and headed inside. They made sure the baby was with them, and then they locked the babysitter out of the house. There she was, on the back porch, banging on the door trying to get in while they watched her from inside.

The babysitter had a slightly different version to tell, of course. And because I am friends with the sitter's mother, I was more than a little mortified. You just don't go around locking the babysitter out of the house, do you?

What my husband likes about the story is this: his sons perceived danger and a lack of justice, and they dealt with it, all on their own.

A few years ago, when I was days away from giving birth to baby Henry, we were at an end-of-the-year banquet for the boys' swim team. At some point after the dinner, two young teenage boys, the resident punks, came to tell me that seven-year-old Charlie had raised his middle finger in their general direction.

I was appalled and quickly heaved myself out of my seat to saunter off in search of my son, bringing Paul with me.

When we found our boy and asked him what in the world he was thinking, he explained that those two much bigger boys had been throwing pinecones at him nonstop. He asked them to stop and they would not. He asked them again, and still they would not stop. Finally he did the one thing he could think of to really send the message, and boy did it ever—they raced right over to his parents to tattle.

My first thought was, *Where in the world did he learn what this meant?* That made me sad. My husband's take, however, was the bigger picture. His son, in a moment of complicated brilliance, figured out how to get these older boys to leave him alone.

In the end, I deferred to my husband. While I certainly don't encourage my boys to act this way, I will begrudgingly admit that it's a step in the direction of slight independence.

With so many sons, I am quick to trust my husband's judgment. Simply put, if I totally ignored his guidance, we might be left with some wimps on our hands.

But everything within reason.

It is Valentine's Day and the boys are sitting on the couch next to my husband.

"We're having a Valentine history lesson," Ethan tells me, and I smile slightly, wondering what lessons of love their father is imparting. I walk out of the room and don't give the lesson another thought.

The next day, I run into the grocery store after church. Paul waits with the boys in the car. When I come back, one of the boys tells me they have finished the lesson—their "Valentine history lesson."

"What have you been discussing?" I ask. Was the lesson

on Cupid, or El Amor, or perhaps all about how Daddy asked Mommy for her hand in marriage on this very day so many years ago? But no, none of those.

It turns out the lesson was about mortal combat. My boys now know all about Braveheart and a certain Valentine's Day massacre.

"This is not exactly what I had in mind," I tell my husband, before he leans in for a kiss and we head home.

The boys are just getting back from a morning trip to the river with friends. Seven-year-old Charlie walks over to show me a cut on his knee.

"Check out this baby," he says with pride.

I gasp. "Are you okay? Do you need a Band-Aid?"

"It's perfectly fine," he assures me. "It's perfectly functional."

He pats me on the shoulder and walks out of the room.

My Boys, My Team

The boys have grown up knowing they are a team. Even if they didn't already think in terms of sports (which they totally do), they have heard it enough everywhere we go.

Whenever we are out in public, someone will invariably come up to us and note that we have all these boys and that I have my own team. Yes, I will say, I am the team mom and my job is to keep the players fed and clothed and prevent them from fouling out.

Before boy number five came along, we were generally limited to being a team needing only four players.

"Oooh," a stranger would coo, "you have your own golf foursome." Another would add that we were halfway to a soccer team or putting a dent in our baseball squad.

I would smile and nod, as long as they didn't mention football.

Once baby Henry was born, we were a basketball team, fair and square. That is the given team and the boys recognize themselves as such.

One day, ten-year-old Elliott asked me if I thought we would be having any more children.

"I'm not sure," I said, not wanting to explain the physics of sagging internal organs and strained coping skills. "Do you think we should?"

"Yes," he said. "Then we could have another little fella to beat up on. And also we could have a sub for the basketball team."

Why Do They Stare at Us?

People will often ask us if we hoped for a girl. Friends and loved ones would also admit they had hoped for one for us. I appreciate their kindness, that they would wish for us something that I'm sure is lovely and wonderful and fun.

Even now, when we are in public, I can feel people's eyes on us. I sometimes imagine they are giving a closer look to the baby to verify that yes, they did, they had another boy. I feel at times that they are sizing me up. "That poor woman," I can hear them say. "She gave it one last shot. And still no girl."

Maybe they're not thinking that at all. Perhaps they're looking because they're curious to see how many there are in that group of boys. Maybe they're staring at us and wondering why they didn't hit the jackpot like me. "Why," they say to themselves, "didn't we wind up with a bunch of boys like that lucky, lucky lady over there?"

Or maybe they're staring because there are boys hanging off the sides of the cart and a few under the cart, and if their mother doesn't turn around right now, that one scaling the shelves to get the box of cookies off the top—he is going to fall.

That, I would imagine, is exactly why they stare.

Safety Measures

We have a family plan in case of emergency—a prearranged meeting place in the event of fire, how the boys should exit the house, where they should go once they are out safely, how to find the safest exit route. These are important bits of information that we try to address without fixating on them.

There are other safety issues we address as well—how to handle a knife, how to walk while carrying a pair of scissors, how to gently close a door so no one loses a finger.

Paul and I are finding we have to clearly spell these things out. I try to imagine what dangerous situations the boys might encounter and work to have a plan in advance for dealing with these in a calm, safe fashion.

One morning as we were getting ready for school, I overheard Paul giving some kind of official safety tip. I walked into the room to find the boys all watching him as he wielded a large, yellow rubber snake.

"If you see someone whipping a snake," he was saying, "you go like this." He then demonstrated how to avoid taking a rubber snake to the face by stepping back when in the line of fire.

Another woman may have balked at this how-to session. And a few years ago that would have been me. What are the odds that anyone would need to know the art of rubber snake defense? While the average person might never have such an object flung in her general direction, I now realize these tidbits of wisdom are the stuff of survival.

Later that day, one of the boys absolutely used that information from his father when he did, in fact, defend himself against a rubber snake attack.

"Tell me about your picture, Ethan."

"Well, this boy is Charlie. And the one next to him is Kevin, and then Billy."

"And who's that on the kite?"

"That's me."

"And where's Elliott?"

"He ran off to call an ambulance."

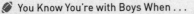

Mysterious Behavior

There are a lot of things about boys that continue to surprise me. I should more accurately say that I continue to surprise myself at the things about boys that keep surprising me. At some point, I should come to accept that this is the way things are. Maybe I'm just in denial.

After all these years of being a mother to boys, I am still caught off guard by their outlook on life, by their approach to simple, easy-to-manage tasks like personal hygiene and using a door to enter the house.

One afternoon I caught eight-year-old Charlie trying to crawl into the house through a slightly opened window. I looked up from the kitchen sink to find his face peering back at me through the window. Accessing this window required crawling on top of the recycling trash can that was situated below, and my son was perched on top of the giant plastic bin, teetering a bit as he grasped the side of the pop-out window.

"No," I said as our eyes met. "Walk around."

"Why?" he asked, keeping his grip and maintaining eye contact.

"Because," I reminded him, "we use doors, not windows, to enter the house."

"But I'm uncivilized," he protested, before hopping off the trash can and going on his way.

This was not the first time I had explained our rules for

coming and going. On a regular basis, I have to tell the boys that the proper way to enter and exit the home is through that rectangular shape with the handle, not a second-story window or an air-conditioning vent or the giant hole they think we should put in the roof—the one that would be perfect for dropping into the house by way of parachute.

"This is what doors were invented for," I explain in response to these ideas. I suspect they think doors are for sissies—who needs a door when there is a perfectly good window right next to it?

The boys' cousins (also boys) came over to play one afternoon, and when they couldn't get the locked door open fast enough, Charlie simply threw open the sash of the dining room window. I looked over just as his cousin was climbing in.

"Why didn't you unlock the door?" I asked my son.

"I couldn't get the key to turn," was his logical explanation.

Comings and goings I understand a bit. I now realize the incredible need and constant search for adventure. Climbing through a window fits the bill. While I don't allow it, it's not so far-fetched as to freak me out.

What I don't understand, what frustrates me to no end, is the total lack of hygienic inclination. Will they outgrow this? I'm clinging to that hope. There will come a time one day, surely, when each of my boys will cross that threshold into the land of self-awareness, and maybe I'll even look back on these days with nostalgia. Is it possible I'll one day miss the times when I would drag my sons kicking and screaming to the bathroom to chip away a week's worth of sludge off their teeth?

I doubt it. Not from a lack of nostalgia, but I have serious reservations about whether that day will come.

One evening we were conducting Personal Hygiene

Night—that evening where we drag out the nail clippers, and Paul and I wrestle the boys to the ground to trim fingers and toes. Elliott was particularly combative and, in a moment of frustration, looked longingly at a brother who wasn't going under the knife.

"How come his nails never grow?" he asked with envy.

"They do grow," I told him. "It's just that he lets me trim his nails on a regular basis."

"Why?" asked my bewildered child.

Why indeed. That this is a valid question in our life explains so much.

RULES I CAN'T BELIEVE I HAD TO MAKE

Seriously, some of the rules around our house are hard to believe. Unless I have everything spelled out, the boys will find ways to push the envelope and possibly harm themselves and those around them in the process.

So in a vain attempt to cover all the bases, I have a running list. It's a combination of things I've read, things I remember from the newspaper or other events, tales of boys and young men doing ridiculous things that caused serious harm or just barely did not—all of those combined with trends I see with my own boys, things I know they will try if I don't outlaw it now.

This list is not posted in our house, but my boys could still recite it to you from memory. That's how often we "review" the list. It goes like this:

1. Boys, you must never crawl into the trunk of someone's car. Even if it is the perfect hiding place and no one will ever look for you there. Even if all the other hiding places have been taken. Even if your brother dares you to climb into this space to see how tough you are. Don't do it. This is a very important rule.

2. Never shut your brother in a refrigerator. I don't care if he says he wants to try it out. That doesn't matter. This rule applies to freezers, dryers, and all other large appliances. Just because your body fits inside any of these items doesn't mean it was meant to be there.

3. Never play with fire. Yes, I know that I liked fire when I was young, maybe even more than you do. I remember that I set fire to the neighbor's doghouse, completely by accident (don't forget that detail), and the best thing I can say about that experience is, now I manage to stay one step ahead of you in the pyromaniacs department. I realize that you are capable of lighting a match and creating a miniature bonfire. I have not forgotten about that time you did just that, oldest son, putting a neat pile of newspapers underneath a perfectly arranged pile of sticks. But just because you can—and in fact already did—make a fire in the backyard does not make it acceptable.

4. Do not open second-story windows. Jumping out of an upstairs window will not result in you flying even though I'm sure you are

convinced it will. No, it will actually end in you breaking something, possibly even worse than that. I don't want to give you details on all the damage a fall like this could do to you. I realize you want details, but the answer is no. It is crucial that you never break this rule, unless of course there is a fire (which you better not have started).

5. Be very careful with power tools, and only use those with permission and when I am in earshot. Don't forget about that time you were using the drill to build your raft. That was all harmless and good until you—yes, I'm looking at you—you went and drilled your hand (and then tried to hide all the blood from me, thinking I would never find out). That hurt, didn't it? A saw would hurt ten times worse.

6. The spray paint rule—don't forget it. Spray paint is only for art projects and can only be used when I say yes and when I'm there to supervise. I'm still a little upset (but yes, I have forgiven you, son) about the time someone celebrated learning the first letter of his name and decorated my entire yard with that letter. And whoever it was that painted the blue tears on the rocking horse out back, well, the horse now looks possessed. So let's not do that again.

7. Do not hogtie your brother and drag him across the yard on the back of your bicycle, even if he claims he is having a blast. That would be dangerous. Even when all parties involved say they are participating freely and without reserve, it is still dangerous. You may, however, hold on to the rope while wearing your rollerblades. I know this doesn't seem like quite as much fun, but trust me. The other method won't end well.

3

Family Togetherness

Pleasing in My Sight

I wish boys were eager to please. If I could change one thing about boys, that would be it.

There are so many days when life would be much easier if the children in my life ached and pined to make me happy—in my perfect little world, they would think first about my reaction to their behavioral choices and then, after that, about their desire to pound their brother.

And yet, when I think about living in a world of sycophant boys, it makes me a little sad. While I'd like everyone to always be perfect, I don't know what I would gain from that. Sure, life would be easy right now, but not down the road. If my boys only toed the line for the sake of it, what good would that be?

Oh, who am I kidding? It would be a ton of good—it would make life perfect, which is exactly what I want and need.

In my perfect dream world, we would go to church, and no one would constantly ask me for a countdown of HOW. MUCH. TIME. IS. LEFT?

In this world, my boys would be eager to dress properly for going out in public. "Why don't we wear golf shirts," they'd say, "instead of these ratty old tees?" They would be willing to get rid of ancient, tattered clothes that are slightly too short and slightly too threadbare. In this world, their father would do the same.

My dream world would be filled with fruits and vegetables. None of those processed foods that currently fill my freezer. Hot Pockets? Who needs 'em? We have carrot sticks and apple slices!

The boys would ask me to trim their nails, instead of hiding their overgrown talons from me. They would never want to leave the house with bed head or untied shoes or while wearing a T-shirt covered with last night's dinner.

It's a tough call, though, and I hate to admit it, but so much of what drives me crazy with boys is what I love most about them as well.

Gifts We Offer

Elliott was hard at work on a school assignment one night, laboring over a classroom contest to see who could find the most words in the phrase "David and Goliath."

He had been working on the project for a while, and he was excited—he was within five words of the girl who had been in the lead on Friday. Every few minutes, he would look up from the paper and ask about a word, wondering if it was an actual word or one he had made up.

"Is *vodta* a word?" he asked at one point. "What is that?"

"I think you mean vodka," I said, explaining it was a clear liquid that grown-ups drink occasionally.

"Is that the stuff you drink in the car on the way to soccer?" he asked. And I explained that, no, I would be arrested for that. He was thinking of Pellegrino.

After a while, Elliott reached his goal—one more word than the girl had on Friday. He was ecstatic. As he was going to bed, I heard him make a comment to Paul.

"This is great," he said. "I love having a writer for a mom."

My boy applauded my ability to distinguish a real word from a made-up one. He saw this as a tremendous gift. As silly as it seems, my heart soared.

With all these boys, I sometimes feel like my strong suits go unnoticed. The things that I am naturally drawn to do are not always things my boys see as any kind of talent—not at this point.

I watch Paul playing with the boys. He is outside with them kicking the soccer ball and shooting hoops, or they are in the front room piled in a wrestling heap. These are things I can join in on, and (except for the wrestling) sometimes do. But these are not the activities I'm always inclined to do.

Even though I love being outdoors as much as the boys do, what I gravitate toward (biking, hiking, appreciating nature) are not the things they gravitate toward (sports their dad likes and shooting stuff). Paul and the boys will do the things I like to do, but it's not always at the top of their list.

Likewise, some things I get excited about are totally off their radar. Around here, there is no one to compliment me on how nice my fall decorations look, no one to tell me my new shoes are really cute. This is absolutely as it should be, of course, but sometimes I notice the absence.

Having said that, I will keep training my boys to articulate that appreciation, to show they care. I will continue to remind them to open the door for me and seat me at the table, and maybe, every so often, pay me a compliment. They learn these things from their father's example, but also from my encouragement. These learned habits are invaluable.

A few weeks ago, as we were walking out the door, I turned to Charlie.

"How do I look?" I asked.

"Like Mom," he replied, and I took it as a compliment of the highest order.

Actions vs. Words

Many Sunday afternoons, we go on a hike as a family. We tend to go to the same trail most weeks, a beautiful nature preserve not far from our home.

At the start of the hike, there are several large silos, left over from when the site was a farm of some sort. One Sunday, as we were about to get on the trail, one of the boys was missing.

"Where's your brother?" I called to the other boys, and as I waited for an answer, I realized that my eyes had instinctively shot up to the top of the silo. I was ruling out possible answers that were unlikely, yet not as unlikely as I'd like to believe.

When did I start to see a silo as a potential safety hazard? Driving by those tall structures for years, I only knew them as the place to store food for farm animals. And then I gave birth to a few boys, and suddenly I see a silo as a magnetic force, drawing my boys into its power. These days it would not shock me to find one of my boys trying to scale the side of one, because they sometimes do.

Our church has several beautiful marble statues. One Sunday, one of the boys walked behind a statue, and my first instinct was to remind him to be sure not to knock that statue over, especially not onto his brother's head.

"Watch out for your brother there," I started, but then stopped. There's no need to say such a thing, right?

Would he knock it over on purpose? you ask. I can't

be sure. I mean, no, of course not, and especially not if his brother was right in front. But there's always that possibility that Detail A (cool, tall statue, fun to knock over) and Detail B (baby brother standing in front of cool statue)—that those two details would not overlap and sound some kind of safety alarm.

I remember reading, when my boys were still very little, about the physiological changes that occur in a boy's brain when he's going through puberty. During that season, the two sides of his brain are literally not touching, which means that the side of the brain that thinks up actions will have very little communication with the side that deals with consequences.

This scares me, not just because this is something I have to look forward to, but because the book seemed to indicate this would be more profound in the teenage years. In our home, this kind of behavior has been going on since our firstborn was a toddler.

Part of the problem has to do with the incredibly creative nature of boys—and that is a wonderful, beautiful gift.

I continue to be amazed, for instance, when I see the wide and varied list of things that a simple stick can become. I see a stick. My boys see a lance, and then a spear, a javelin, or possibly a high jump pole. Later on it's a fishing pole and the world's skinniest rocket. And that's just the first ten minutes.

Seemingly harmless objects somehow become weapons in the hands of a boy, and it's a full-time job keeping track of what they are working on now. In order to cover all my bases, I would basically have to lock the boys in a room with only a handful of marshmallows and a few popsicle sticks to play with.

But I spoke too soon, because everyone knows that popsicle sticks are some of the best weapons on the market.

Truthfully, if I take this attitude, it won't get them far. I have to allow my boys to be who God created them to be—to enjoy that sense of adventure, that free spirit that wants to explore everything in their path. I'll do my best, as their mother, to remind them what adventures are smart, and pray God finds a balance between my desire to protect them and their desire to have some fun.

Brotherly Love

Around here, love doesn't always look the way I'd like it to look.

Of course my boys can be very sweet with me—they are always quick to give me a kiss (on the lips even!), to tell me they love me. I get fresh-picked flowers (from the neighbor's yard), and if I'm feeling sad, at least one of the boys will ask if I'm okay.

Even with their father, my sons are very affectionate. My husband does a wonderful job of extending hugs and kisses, of being quick to tell his boys, and me, that he loves us.

Boys can certainly be tender.

But when it comes to brotherly love, I'm finding the manifestations are often strange and curious. Between brothers, love hurts.

One of the biggest outlets for brotherly affection is wrestling, a sport that is wildly popular in our home. I can always tell when the boys are happy and excited, because they are wound up in a giant ball of frenzy in the front room. Wrestling is how our household gets revved up in the morning and winds down in the evening—it is our cup of coffee and nightcap rolled into one.

In our home, we also have a lot of high fives, which I think down the road will turn into the manly hug. My boys already hug me and Dad and grandparents and relatives. But amongst themselves, they still stick to the high five. They use it in times of utter joy and of consolation. It's a really useful tool—not too much of a commitment but more meaningful than just a smile. I recently caught myself high-fiving a friend when we were discussing a book I really liked. The boys are totally rubbing off on me.

Between the brothers, there are also slaps on the bum and noogies and ninja kicks. These all sound iffy, and it's true they can turn bad in an instant. If someone is feeling slightly happy but also slightly agitated, the ninja kick can go downhill quickly. I keep a close eye on some of these methods of affection, or before I know it, a moment of joy turns into a moment of pain.

Then there are words of encouragement.

In my female world, we say things like "You are amazing" and "I know you can do it!" Being a nurturer, I work hard to offer words that will encourage and inspire. I want my dear ones to know the depths of my love and that I am thinking of them. As a woman, I have an urge to share the special moments.

For guys, it's a bit different.

One Sunday morning, Ethan was an altar server at our church. Because he had to prepare, we dropped him off at the back door of the church early.

As he was walking away from the car, Charlie called out to his brother.

"Go get 'em, tiger!"

In other words: You are amazing. I know you can do it!

"What are we shooting at?" asks one boy excitedly.

"I don't know," answers another, "but keep shooting!"

Trying for the Girl?

I was paying my bill at a restaurant one day, holding baby Henry as I signed my receipt.

"Is that your first baby?" asked the cashier.

"No," I answered, "it's our fifth. This guy is the youngest of five boys."

"You didn't want any girls?" asked the woman, and I held back from explaining it doesn't really work that way.

I get this all the time, of course, and I know people mean well. I have gotten over feeling agitated when people ask me if I'm going to try for "my girl." The universe doesn't owe me a daughter, I'm inclined to say. But I realize they don't need a lesson in biology. They are just curious, and I probably would be too.

No one sets out to have a single-gender sibling set. Plenty of people get some of each. The rest of us wind up with something that looks different than what we imagined but is somehow the answer to the hopes and dreams we never knew we had.

It's true I have moments when I wonder about having a daughter. One day I was riding with two of my childhood friends, women I have known since I was a girl. One of them noted she was planning to teach her daughter to shave her legs soon, and I got a little lump in my throat, just for a second.

I remember learning to shave with these very women,

some twenty years earlier. I have shared so many life experiences with these dear friends, and now I watch as they share those same rites of passage with their daughters. In these moments, I think that having a daughter would be so nice. I look at a picture of myself as a girl and sometimes think it would be sweet to have a little more *me* in my life.

But then I look at my boys, these gifts God has given me, and I try to decide which one I would have opted to trade for a girl. Most days, I can't come up with the answer to that question.

It is not simply about being a mother who has sons or daughters, or even some of each. The journey of motherhood centers on being the person God has chosen out of all humanity and space and time to care for these souls, these beings who will exist for all eternity.

The thought of that incredible task, that humbling honor, is more than enough to direct my focus back to an overwhelming gratitude for the gift of my children, my incredible sons, in my life.

Etiquette

One afternoon, eight-year-old Charlie was standing in the doorway of the laundry room. Suddenly, he turned his back to me, stuck out his behind, and loudly passed gas. Before I could chide him for such rude behavior, he invited me to do the same.

"Do you think you could do that, Mom?" he asked.

"Charlie," I said, "mothers don't play that with their sons."

"Do they play it with their friends?"

I'm not sure how long it will take until this boy learns that most ladies don't roll like that. I hope he won't be too disappointed.

Guilty as Charged

I can hear it loud and clear.

Someone is crying, but mad crying, not hurt crying. I go outside to check and find Augie lying face up in the tipped-backward running stroller. He is upset because someone walked up behind him and told him to get buckled and then, without further ado, tilted him until the back of the stroller was resting on the ground.

"He said, 'Are you buckled?'" recounts Augie. "And then he said, 'Well, you better get buckled.'"

This is all relayed to me with the appropriately menacing tones, and I can tell that the real issue is not that the boy got tipped over onto his back, but that his older brother treated him with a total lack of grace and courtesy.

"Did you talk to him in an ugly fashion?" I ask the offending party.

"Pretty ugly," the offender admits with a nod.

I can't stay mad for long—that boy came clean remarkably quick. And he was even willing to quantify just how ugly his tone had been.

What Are They Thinking?

It is late afternoon and the boys are discussing worst-case scenarios, trying to determine which would be the greater of two evils and how they would decide.

"Which would you rather . . . ?" says one boy, and I listen as he puts forth two options and the group of them discusses which they would choose. The options are generally gross and grosser, or bad and worse. There is never a clear-cut winner, and I guess that's the point of the game.

At one point, they include me in the discussions.

"Do you think it would be worse to be stabbed in the throat," asks Elliott, "or be forced to eat poo?"

"I don't even want to think about that," I say with disgust.

A while later, he comes up to me again.

"Which would be worse," he asks, "to be forced to shoot a bald eagle or to have diarrhea for the rest of your life?"

"I'm hoping neither," I say, encouraging him to change the subject. He insists the game will be helpful if we are ever in dire straits and need to make a tough decision.

I appreciate their desire to hash out the serious issues of life with fervor. I'm hoping, however, that none of these discussions will ever come in handy.

"Is that an insult or a compliment?" the boy asks sincerely.
It's not a rhetorical question. He really wants to know.

Artistic Endeavors

One of my great mothering joys to date has been watching my boys perform in their school plays. So far, each boy has earned a hearty role in his play, and even though we're talking elementary school productions, I still treasure these moments.

Acting is one of the few things I can take credit for when it comes to my offspring. With boys, it's only natural to give the father credit for just about everything—the good and the bad. The boys got their broad shoulders and lanky build from their father, as well as their ability to spend half an hour using the restroom. Like Dad, they enjoy playing basketball and memorizing sports statistics. They also read the books he used to read, and dress in a fashion that looks just like the pictures from his youth.

I gave birth to my husband's clones—five of them.

Very few boys go around advertising that they got their looks or athletic abilities from their mom. Even if it's true, and Mother was a tremendous athlete, it just doesn't seem to work that way. Credit can't always go where it is due.

So I offer the ability to emote—this is my genetic contribution. As I watch my boys up onstage, acting, I take pride in knowing that they get that from me—whether they like it or not.

One afternoon Elliott came home from school terribly excited. He had been cast as the lead in his fourth-grade play.

"We're doing Om, Om . . . Omelet!" he exclaimed.

"Do you mean *Hamlet*?" I asked. Yes, he said, that was it. The class was performing *Hamlet*, and he was Hamlet.

I try to avoid getting overly involved when the boys are memorizing their lines—if they notice I'm worked up, they will retreat. I tread carefully, walking the fine line that separates a happy, involved momma from Stage Mother. I am not a stage mother. I am not a stage mother.

It's fun to help the boys rehearse their lines, to work on costumes and talk about delivery and timing. I just can't get carried away. I'm afraid they might run in the other direction, or worse, give their father credit for this as well.

Why Love and Pain Look Alike

One afternoon I was working on dinner while the boys played in the backyard. At least five times, I ran to the window after hearing moaning, wailing, and terrifying shrieks, only to discover each time that the boys were merely having fun.

At one point, I heard Charlie screaming in agony. I banged on the window because his oldest brother was sitting on him. As I stood in the window demanding that Ethan stop, he looked up at me with a wide grin across his face. I eyed him in disbelief.

"How dare he just look at me while he's torturing his brother," I muttered. I threw my dishtowel on the counter, and just as I was about to march outside, the younger boy peeked out from his brother's armpit. Charlie smiled broadly, and it was obvious he was having at least as much fun as everyone else.

A few minutes later, there was more wailing. This time I saw Augie lying on his stomach, his arms behind his back. I couldn't tell if his wrists were actually tied to each other or if he was somehow holding them perfectly still. A few feet away, Elliott dangled from the top of the swing set, his hands gripping tight while his younger brother tried in earnest to grab onto his feet. More wailing, followed by more laughter, and once again I realized it was all in good fun.

I shut the kitchen window after that, deciding to just base my decision making on sight alone. It seems I'm not much of an expert in the art of verbal nuance. The shrieks of joy and sadness, I am learning, are only one Indian burn apart.

Seventy-Four Minutes . . .
but Who's Counting?

The funniest thing . . . one morning I told the three big boys they could each have a friend over after school. I think I must have been experiencing a serious post-exercise endorphin high, and also a bit of Crazy. If I'm remembering that morning correctly, it also didn't look like it was going to be cold and rainy. My vision of the afternoon consisted of the backyard and bike riding and fun in the great outdoors.

But the afternoon rolled around and the weather was gloomy and not quite right for being outdoors. And the funny thing about when my boys have friends over is that it always involves more boys!

I stared at the afternoon ahead and realized for more than an hour (but less than two) there would be eight boys in my house.

This should be interesting, I thought to myself. It would probably also be overwhelming, but perhaps less intimidating if it also involved my having a glass of wine. But for some reason I don't think that would really qualify as Responsible Parenting.

(P.S. I wasn't really intimidated. Not once I started hiding in the closet, anyway.)

The afternoon of the playdate went something like this:

3:56 p.m.—The last of the three boys arrives. Charlie is being very good about including younger brother Augie.

4:02 p.m.—Baby Henry wants to be included as well. But they are playing LEGOs. I put Henry in his jumpy seat so he can be part of the scene without ingesting it.

4:06 p.m.—Charlie: "Now I'm getting bored. Don't worry, I'm getting something to eat."

4:07 p.m.—Friend #3: "I'm starving! My mom wouldn't let me have anything to eat."

4:08 p.m.—Me: "Let's not walk through the house eating, please."

4:08 p.m.—Friend #3 walks through the house, over to me. He is eating a granola bar. He shows me the LEGO ship he made; it's pretty cool.

4:09 p.m.—Charlie: "What do you want to do now, old chum?"

4:13 p.m.—Charlie and Friend #3 invite Elliott and Friend #2 to play Medieval Times outside in the damp. Friend #3 isn't exactly sure what that means, he admits, but they bundle up to give it a shot.

4:13 p.m.—Ethan and Friend #1 are waiting upstairs to "bombard." Ethan's bed is covered with plastic swords and guns. And also all of his Valentine's candy.

4:15 p.m.—Twenty minutes in and I'll admit it's going just fine. It's so much calmer than when they were toddlers and we'd have playdates.

4:18 p.m.—Charlie and his buddy walk into the study with

a bag of Cheetos. "The kitchen," I declare, "is now closed."

4:21 p.m.—I am freezing. I hand wash all the dishes from snack time. The water warms me up. I walk away from the sink to find the back door wide open. No wonder I'm cold.

4:22 p.m.—Ethan and Friend #1 run through the kitchen wielding lightsabers.

4:28 p.m.—"We need to get ready for war," Charlie declares, running to his room. "We need weapons, weapons, weapons!"

4:30 p.m.—"There's this guy," Elliott says, walking in from the garage, "who can do the pogo stick on the handles." I nip that thought in the bud. He smiles, like he's starting to understand where I'm coming from. It's enough that he jumps without holding on to the handles; I draw the line at him standing on them.

4:33 p.m.—A war is breaking out in the playroom. Henry is stuck in the middle.

4:37 p.m.—Elliott and Friend #2 are each bent over a paper towel covered with a small mound of white crystalline, which they are licking. "Throw that away," I tell them. "You don't need to be eating salt." "It's not salt," they assure me. "It's sugar." Even better.

4:45 p.m.—"Fight like a maaaaan," someone yells in the distance. I linger for an extra moment in the bathroom and note I'm having a good hair day.

4:54 p.m.—Henry is gnawing on someone's discarded

school sock. He puts it down before I even reach him. Smart kid.

4:58 p.m.—T minus 17 minutes. I treat myself to a Dove's Promises (dark chocolate). "Test your own limits," it tells me, "and keep going."

5:03 p.m.—Time to round them up and clean up the playroom. "Soldiers of War," I bellow from the bottom of the stairs, "to your post!"

5:10 p.m.—Everyone gets a snack. We load up. "This is a day," says Charlie to Friend #3, "that we will remember to our graves."

A wonderful adventure indeed.

What You See Is What You Get

Maybe I watch too many mystery shows, but I'm often tempted to think that circumstances and events always involve deep-seated issues, that there is always more going on than meets the eye. One summer, my son spent weeks with bloodshot eyes. I started wondering at what point I should call the doctor, concerned that he had a major infection, or worse, that he was walking around fighting back tears because he was sad about something.

One day we were swimming laps, and he mentioned that his goggles didn't seem to work properly. After a little investigative work, we discovered that they were leaking and my son simply could not figure out how to tighten them. I adjusted the strap. Eyes cleared up. That was the end of that.

I tend to overcomplicate things.

As a woman, I often feel like it's my job to make things ten times more difficult than they need to be. I'm not trying to cause problems. It's just my nature.

Oddly enough, when I overanalyze and talk things out and think ad nauseam about who and what and why—well, that's usually just my way of simplifying things.

"I think," I'll tell my husband in a discussion, "what you really mean is . . ." and then I'll offer him my best analytical services. Usually he will have to explain that, no, that's not what he really means. What he really means is exactly what he just said the first time.

The nice thing is that my husband has been able to more or less explain this phenomenon to me. He uses very short sentences, like: I mean what I say. The end.

"Are you sure you don't mean that what you really feel is . . ." and off I go with another brilliant analysis of his complicated behavior.

"No," he will say, and refer me back to Explanation A.

So now I'm starting to believe my husband when he tells me this, which has the added benefit of helping me better understand my boys as well. I'm still not totally there (could it really be that simple? I don't believe it), but I am getting more comfortable with the idea of listening to the words they say, instead of what I think the words should be.

When it comes to feelings, my boys almost always say what they mean. That doesn't mean they are constantly emoting. But when they do have something to say, they say it. When my boys are sad, they tell me. When they are scared, they tell me. When they are angry, they hit the person who wronged them and I'll hear about that too.

That boys put it all out there is a blessing and a curse. I'm glad to be in the loop, but when my boys get upset, they don't hold it in. They don't wait until a more appropriate time to calmly deal with frustrations—if one boy gets upset with his brother, he will belt him one and then move on.

As a woman, I find this way of relating absolutely intriguing. Could I really make my life that carefree, I wonder, by simply dealing with something as soon as it happens? Of course, I don't think slugging every person who irks me is the answer, but there has to be an aspect of this that is so healthy and good. With boys, after a problem is dealt with, it is in the past, and past grievances rarely come up again.

The challenging aspect of this nature is the issue of propriety—raising a healthy boy is not the same as raising a healthy bear cub. While a boy's nature may very well be to instantly deal with his aggravations, he must learn that there is a time and a place for everything. I don't care if your brother just elbowed you for no good reason—you don't punch him in the arm during church. No! Wrong! Unacceptable! (I'm also learning that short sentences are the most effective.)

While it's great that the problem will be over after that retaliatory punch, doing it in church is never a good idea. In that case, it's better to wait. Many are the tales I could tell about the boys taking matters into their own hands in the most inappropriate moments. I am proud of you for being self-reliant, I want to say, but save it for when nobody's watching.

The downside of this "healthy" nature of boys is the total lack of pride I am able to retain in my life. Too often have I been floating along feeling like the Queen of the World, that I have perfected the art of parenting boys, only to be greeted by the sight of one boy slugging another in front of God and (worse) my mother. I will never give speeches on mild-mannered males.

But ask me about humility, because I get lots of chances to work on that. I can tell you all about how you must have high standards for your boys, with the understanding that you might never reach perfection. What a challenge to be a woman, with a woman's feelings and ideals, working to raise tomorrow's men—men who will be manly and strong and also respectful.

Part of me is learning to let go of my pride—as a mother,

I continue to hold my boys to high standards. But I'm in constant discussions with my husband about the nature of those standards: Are they realistic for a family of boys? Are they too high? Or worse, are they too low?

Even more importantly, I'm trying to reach that place where I don't see it as a personal failure when we arrive at a point that is lower than our aim.

I aim high—and wear dark glasses in public.

"Get mine for me," Charlie tells his brother. "You are my humble slave."

Talk Is Cheap

There was a time when I would fret about communication with my sons. When they were young, I worried that I would miss chances to have heartfelt talks with them. Before I was a mother, I imagined that I would spend evenings with my children seated at the foot of my bed—they would hang on to my every word as I explained all about life and love and the mysteries of the universe.

Then I had five sons.

Now I realize that every moment of the day is an opportunity for communication, but that taking advantage of these moments requires finesse and aplomb.

My initial approach to communication was over-the-top, loud, and rambling speeches to drive the point home. One day my husband advised me that this approach was terribly ineffective, pointing out that if he didn't respond well to that method, why should our prepubescent boys?

One of the places we have the best conversations as a family is in the car. Growing up, this was always my mom and dad's approach to talking with us kids—they would take out one or two of us to get a soda, and then we'd drive around.

My parents learned early on that being in the car provided a laid-back feel, because facing forward is much less intense than facing each other. That approach fostered many wonderful and heartfelt discussions.

I had forgotten about their approach until I realized that same phenomenon was happening with my own little family. When the boys and I run errands, I began to notice, we always seem to have wonderful discussions.

At first I saw it as kind of a fluke—we would load up to do our shopping and would end up having these great little talks. While we weren't always solving all the world's problems, the boys were opening up, taking the time to explore their thoughts and feelings, and then *sharing those thoughts and feelings* with me. I felt like the luckiest woman alive.

Eventually I put it all together and realized I needed to take advantage of these times. I started being more proactive with our driving time, using it to sometimes subtly bring up a topic I wanted to discuss without getting up on my soapbox and immediately sending them running—both physically and mentally.

One summer afternoon, the walls were closing in on me. We were in our third day of 100-degree weather, and the high temperatures coupled with our status of having a one-year-old were leaving us with very little to do. Even going to the pool was out, because I was afraid Henry would wilt in the humidity.

After book time and game time and a family work party followed by back-to-back episodes of *Tom and Jerry*, we needed to get out. We might not be able to be outside, I declared, but we could definitely be out of the house.

Our first stop, I decided, would be at our favorite gas station. I loaded the boys and we headed in that direction. When we arrived, I directed the boys to the walk-in beer cooler, which is kept at a refreshingly crisp 28 degrees. We all stepped inside and stood for a minute.

"This feels awesome," someone declared. "Let's never leave." I'm not sure, but I think that person may have been me.

We had to leave eventually of course, and I told the boys they could each spend two dollars on a treat. While I know that sounds like a lot, I felt the boys had earned it—they had done chores for several hours that morning, and I figured fifty cents an hour is legal in some countries. I also decided the eight dollars total would be money well spent, because I wasn't sure where we were headed after our first stop, but I knew it would involve riding in the car. A nice quiet ride would be just the ticket.

After each boy made his selections, we loaded back up. I was armed with an ice-cold fountain soda and a pack of Fig Newtons to share with Henry, and everyone else had a plethora of Coke slushes and five-cent candies. It was then that I should have calculated that the grams of sugar being ingested would be indirectly proportional to the amount of quiet I would experience for the rest of our outing. Deep down, though, I didn't care—we were out of the house!

We headed down the road to our city's quiet airport. The boys wanted to see a plane take off, and just as we approached, one of the boys spotted one. We cruised along a side road and followed the plane as it slowly taxied. Then it turned, so we turned. We followed it back until we realized it was slowing down, not speeding up, and it was actually heading to the terminal.

Somehow in the midst of all this, we got to talking about religion and being Catholic and where exactly did the Catholic faith come from. The boys were so talkative, so interested in the history of our faith, and as we drove along, I was thankful for these beautiful moments that God provides. I could not have planned a better conversation.

"What about the Jews?" asked eight-year-old Charlie after a minute. "What do they believe?"

"They don't believe Jesus is the actual Messiah they had been waiting for," I told him. "They believe he was a prophet."

"But what if they're right?" Charlie wondered. "How do you know?"

I started to mentally flip through my history and theology to come up with a suitable answer, until my six-year-old answered for me.

"She knows because she's Mom," Augie said, exasperated, "and Mom knows everything."

How Did I Get Here?

One evening I was finishing some transactions on the computer. I had won some items on an online auction site and started to write an email to the seller.

"Dear Sir," I typed, "I am the winning bidder of your set of neo-classic Star Wars figures . . . ," and before I could write any more, I pushed myself back from the computer with a startle and took a deep breath.

Then I started to laugh. I called a friend and told her what I had just done, about the strange turn my life had just taken.

"How do I even know what a 'neo-classic Star Wars figure' is?" I marveled. Up until then, those were the kinds of things reserved for my brothers and their friends. I certainly paid no attention to what spaceships flew in the Alliance Fleet or who belonged to the evil Galactic Empire.

Now I can tell you who reigns supreme in Middle Earth, and where you can buy a good carabiner clip, and maybe even what kind of gas mileage you can get in a rebel starship.

None of this happened overnight, of course, but that day, as I wrote those words to secure those Star Wars figures, I knew my life had shifted, that I was heading into new territory. I was a little afraid, but mostly just curious.

At that moment, as I sat and laughed with my friend at the craziness of life with boys, I could scarcely imagine all the adventure and joy waiting for me. The purchase of these little plastic figures was just one of a million new life experiences waiting for me in my journey of motherhood.

I could never have predicted that I would be a woman who could hear her child screaming and decide to just wait it out and see whether that shriek is legit. I had no idea I could learn to care so much about the plight of the dinosaur and how they felt when they became extinct. I'm also shocked to find myself hiding the "good food" in oversized boxes of bran flakes and how pleased I am for trying that approach.

Mostly, though, I didn't realize what mission motherhood would become, especially in raising these boys. What an incredible duty I have as a mother of boys—the sweet, impish creatures in my care today are the men of tomorrow. The weight of the world is indeed on my shoulders.

One morning the boys and I had to go to the mall to get uniform pants, something I try to keep stocked much like milk or corn dogs.

As I stood in line to pay, a woman in front of me was buying several pairs of Levi's. She turned to me as she finished paying.

"Are all those boys yours?" she asked, her nose wrinkling as she spoke.

"Yes!" I said. My reply was too enthusiastic, but I could tell by the look on her face this interaction might require my enthusiasm to balance her negativity.

"I don't know how you do it," she said. "I can barely handle my boys and I only have two."

That wasn't as bad as I thought, not like the time the woman at the school supply store had made an editorial on the boys' wild behavior.

"I'll bet you are *really* tired at the end of the day," she had commented, and I tried to pretend like my head wasn't going to explode.

That day, the boys kept making a break for the automatic doors, and each time I would gently guide them back to the cart.

"Keep your hand on *this*," I'd say, placing a boy's palm on the edge of the counter.

"They're actually being much worse than normal," I said to the woman. Why try to bunt with small talk when I can just state the obvious and hit it out of the park?

Yes, I'm tired at the end of the day, I wanted to say, What mother isn't? So my children are pretending that their superpowers are opening the doors and that, once open, the boys must leap into the air and assail the bad guy with their bionic leg-strength. Why should that make me more tired than the next mom?

We women with boys (and it's a heck of a lot of us, really), we need to encourage each other. Yes, it's tough. Yes, boys can be wild. But it's worth it. You're doing great. You're going to make it.

You are raising tomorrow's men. Make warriors, not wimps.

Elliott had recently lost a tooth, and he was convinced he'd been robbed by the Tooth Fairy.

"I'm sure the Tooth Fairy didn't steal your tooth," I said in a haze that morning. (The Tooth Fairy's newborn had been keeping her awake.) I persuaded him to try again.

Sure enough, the next morning the boy came downstairs with his monetary prize, and also a note. ("Be grateful," wrote the Tooth Fairy, "for all your blessings.")

"What did the Tooth Fairy bring you?" I asked.

"Hate mail."

Neighbors Next Door

For a long time, there was a black spot on the side of our garage. From far away, it looked like a smudge of dirt. Up close, however, it was clearly a large chunk of nothing—a spot where the siding has been damaged, smashed a bit, and broken off. One afternoon, the boys had been shooting their bows and arrows in the backyard; someone missed the target, pretty significantly, and for the longest time the side of my house wanted to tell it to the world. There is now a cute little birdfeeder that hangs lower than it should to house a bird, but does the trick of covering the hole.

Some of these antics make me worry about our neighbors—not about their safety, but about their level of tolerance. After all these years, however, they are all still so good to us. They all seem to genuinely enjoy my boys as much as I do, and I'm always touched and grateful for their generous love (and patience). "Aunt" Cathy and her mother, Miss Charlotte, who live right next door, tell friends their favorite Friday evening activity is sitting on their screened porch listening to our boys play in the backyard.

It doesn't hurt that across the backyard live my parents, and on most days this arrangement is perfect. My boys love to slip away and spend a few minutes with Gramma and Papa. "I'm going over for a visit," one boy will say, and comes home twenty minutes later with a handful of candy. The boys walk next door to ask my dad about a bug or to help with his garden. My mom and I will chat at the fence while the boys shoot hoops in the driveway.

My husband is actually quite supportive of this setup as well. He grew up next door to his own grandparents and remembers those years fondly. He recognizes the beauty of a back-door grandparent relationship.

There are some days, however, when I wonder if we are too close for comfort—their comfort, not ours. Though my mother grew up with seven brothers and raised five boys of her own, she cannot stand to hear stories about my boys if those stories involve fast speeds or high jumps or getting too far out in the ocean.

One afternoon I got a call.

"Hi, Rach," said the voice at the other end, "it's Mom."

"Hey, Mom," I said. "What's going on?"

"Rach," she said, "I waited as long as I could to call. But I can't take it anymore."

She went on to explain that for the last two or three or five hundred hours, she had been looking at a contraption set up by my boys on their swing set. When my mother is sitting in her breakfast nook, looking out her kitchen windows, this swing set is in her direct view. Most days this would not bother her. But on this day, she was seeing something very distracting and also potentially harmful.

"There is a brick tied to a rope, just dangling in the air," she explained. She said she had been watching that setup for a while, and finally the thought of a hand or foot or face getting smashed by that thing was more than she could take. "Would you take it down?" she finally mustered. "I'm afraid someone is going to get really hurt."

I walked into the backyard, and indeed, there it was: a

brick dangling in the air a few feet above the ground. Horribly dangerous, but also pretty clever. The boys explained they were waiting for some kind of animal to scamper through and then they'd release the brick to catch their prey.

Unfortunately, they had lost interest and moved on to something else. And dear sweet Gramma was left to sit and wait and worry.

Even with all those sons and brothers, my mother has always been much more safety conscious than I. Which was probably a built-in mechanism for my sanity.

Several years ago, my brother came over to take my boys fishing. It was a lazy summer afternoon, and he was a college student with nothing to do. The boys had been hard at work for several days on some homemade fishing poles. Up in their rooms, they had created an arsenal of rods using large sticks from the backyard, fishing line from Papa's collection, hooks, and, of course, duct tape.

My brother went upstairs to help the boys gather up their things to head out and fish. He came downstairs a few minutes later.

"Rach," he stammered, "you're . . . it's . . ." And then he finally got it out. "Mom would have never let us have fishing hooks in our room."

That might make me seem cool or open-minded or really, really chilled out, but it mostly just proves the point that my mother is a much more savvy woman than I.

"Are there any odd goings-on?" asks six-year-old Augie as he walks into the room.

Well, let's see, I think to myself. There's your baby brother who keeps climbing on the dining room table trying to swing from the chandelier. There's Charlie tied up in a blanket, being dragged by Elliott, who is declaring him the victim of a very large, deadly spi-

Family Togetherness 🏈

der. "He has been stung by She-lob," says Elliott sadly. And where is Ethan? Oh yes, he is standing in the front room trying to spin a plate on a skinny wooden stick.

"Nope," I tell Augie as I survey the scene, "no odd goings-on. Nothing out of the ordinary here at all."

STUFF I SAY THAT NO LONGER
SOUNDS CRAZY (TO ME)

- "I am *not* a wrestling mat."
- "No, you may not, and if I find a knife stuck in my kitchen cutting board, you will be in very big trouble."
- "Stay off the roof."
- "Why are there blocks of wood cooking in my oven?"
- "While that is indeed a clever invention, you will never be able to fly." (Is this one mean? I can't decide. It feels like a moral dilemma of finding the space where justice and mercy kiss. I don't want their spirits to be crushed. But I think it's even more important that their bones stay intact too.)
- "You can try to invent a jet pack, but I will not buy the fuel for it."
- "What do you mean you *accidentally* kicked your brother in the lip?"
- "Wear something nice, like a T-shirt with no stains on it."
- "Your aim is very good, but you are not to shoot at the newspaper when I'm holding it up to read. I don't care if it's only a Nerf bullet. Never again."

4

The Other Heroes
in Our House

My Husband, the Boy Scout

We are into Boy Scouts. I wouldn't call us hard-core—we
don't have Scout pillowcases or anything—but we have a lot
of boys who all do Scouts, and that fact elevates our family
to expert status simply by default.

My boys are natural-born Boy Scouts. This stems less from
a nature that is always prepared and has more to do with their
inherent love of fire and wild behavior. If you have a passion
for fire and for being wild, you will make a very fine Scout.

When my husband was considering whether we would be
a family of Boy Scouts, I wasn't totally supportive. I vaguely
remember my brothers' adventures with Scouts, and while
it seemed like they had plenty of fun, I was reluctant mostly
out of a fear of overcommitting.

When our oldest son was ready to start Scouts, we were
trying to juggle him and his three younger brothers, learning
to manage school and sports and religious classes, while still
finding peace in our home life. Throwing Scouts into the mix
seemed risky at best.

"If we do Scouts," I told my husband, "it has to be your
thing. You and the boys. I can't commit to anything else."

My husband agreed to those conditions and off we went
on our Scouting adventure.

I was pleased with my stipulation and did a good job of
keeping my involvement to a minimum. After all, most of the

outings and projects are geared for boys to enjoy with their dad, their grandpa, or some other non-female type. If you are a female who enjoys being in charge of ten seven-year-old boys who are learning to tie a square knot, way to go—you are one in a million.

The times we host a Scout meeting at our house, I love watching my husband lead the group—from my vantage point in the kitchen, far away from the madness.

But over the years I have realized that I can't be totally uninvolved in this extracurricular activity. There are some things, even with Scouting, that take a feminine touch.

Charlie came to me one evening, upset about the state of his Scout uniform.

"You never sew on any of my patches," he sighed, and went on to demonstrate how all his Scouting buddies had decked-out shirts with every single award they had received. "They're all 'check me out, look how good I look,'" said my boy, "and I have nothing."

I couldn't argue with him there. As part of my resolve to keep my distance, I had never taken the time to figure out where the patches went on the shirt. It was all so overwhelming. It seemed like every few weeks, someone was coming home with some new, very nice-looking something or other that needed to be added to some section of the uniform. But where? And how could I find this information?

While I had never made a resolution to abandon the patches and awards, the thought of dealing with it was just terribly daunting. Instead of putting the patches and shirts in an obvious place where I would remember to research and then deal with the situation, I would tuck it all away, out of sight and out of mind.

To my credit, it's not like I was throwing anything away.

I had a very lovely basket designated for keeping track of all the awards—Pinewood Derby patches, decals for major accomplishments, special pins for Scout camp and service projects. They were all there together, just waiting for the day when I would suddenly decide that this was a priority in my life, right after I planned this month's menu and painted the baseboards in the playroom closets.

And then that night, when I saw the frustration on Charlie's face, I realized the time had come. I might have decided that Scouting was not my deal, but a mother can never say never.

So that's one romantic moment of Scouts, when I rose to the challenge and met the needs of my precious little boy. It was lovely, and I felt really good.

Now let me tell you about real-life Scouting stuff, and how I hide out in my bedroom when we host a meeting.

Each of our boys is in a different pack. The groups meet on alternating Mondays, and Paul takes turns going to their meetings. While each pack has an official leader, the dads take turns hosting and leading the meetings.

It is Monday, and all day the note on my calendar has been taunting me. Scouts here tonight! Scouts here tonight!

On this particular day, when it is our turn to host, I keep reading the note hoping the message will change. But it does not, and just after dinner, the boys begin to arrive. As soon as my other boys are settled, whether at their own Scout meeting or crashing this gathering at our house, I make sure my husband has the pack under control before I retreat to my room.

A few minutes later, there are loud noises outside my bedroom door. It is the sound of little boys wrestling. Or maybe they're really fighting—I can't tell the difference. But the men are in charge, my husband and the other dads who are here for the meeting, and I'm off the clock! I stay in my happy place and refrain from investigating.

But it's killing me, and I wonder if I should really just sit back and not intervene.

Suddenly the madness stops.

"Oh man," I hear a boy say, "I'm really bleeding."

"You are?"

There is the sound of feet shuffling. The bathroom door opens, the injured goes off to inspect. The bleeder returns and playing (or is it fighting?) resumes.

Meanwhile, there is the sound of dads talking in the kitchen. I wonder why they don't come in and calm down all this crazy. But it's Scouts, not my domain. I'm not here to henpeck. I'm only here because hiding in my bedroom is as far away as I can get. There is nowhere else to go.

It is 8:10 and someone is saying the words I've been longing to hear.

"Get your jacket," says a dad. "It's time to leave."

Ten minutes late. Not that I'm counting.

A friend calls in the midst of this, and I tell her about my woes.

"I'm a very tired prisoner in my own home," I whisper while hiding under the covers.

"Is it from 7 to 9?" she asks.

"No," I tell her, "just an hour."

"So it's all the boys in all the troops then?" she asks, and I have to admit that it's just the five other boys in this particular troop. Then she does the math and points out this is six boys for one hour. I concur with her arithmetic.

Suddenly, she seems less sympathetic.

I'm not quite sure why this is so difficult for me, why a little extra noise for a few extra minutes with a couple of extra boys—what's the big deal? I handle five boys every day. We only host Scouts at our house every few months, and it overwhelms me every single time.

Simply put, it's the combination. Scouts often brings out the WILD in boys. And on a day when I have been watching the clock for the baby's 7 p.m. bedtime (Because he needs it. Bad.) I feel like I'm just biding my time until it's quiet and everyone can go to bed. I finally put Henry down, despite the chaos, because having him awake in a puddle of fatigue is worse than trying to bed him in the middle of this hurricane.

Sometimes I get frustrated with myself for what I see as an inability to cope, to roll with the punches for this one short, little hour. But it's a challenge at the end of a long day to give of myself when I feel I have nothing left to give. I think too that what is most frustrating is that I'm not in charge, and I must sit back and let other people run the show. As a mom, that concept is both rare and challenging.

The great irony of motherhood is that while you sometimes long for someone else to be in charge, it is next to impossible to mentally accept that reality.

Even when the Scouts leave that evening, my boys are still pumped. They play tunes as they pass the piano, and they are gearing up for a game of two-on-two basketball in the playroom. They need to go to bed.

And then, it is my husband to the rescue. He is totally winning points with me by sending the boys in to kiss me good night. He is rounding them up, quieting them down, and finally here is the air of calm I have been waiting for.

It's not so bad to let someone else run the show after all.

Calvin, Our Fearless Leader

One spring afternoon, the boys and I were talking about summer reading, discussing what books they've read and what books they might try to tackle that summer. Each boy would read some exceptional piece of great literature, I explained, and then present a report to the rest of the family.

I had been researching the plethora of classics that little boys love—tales of shipwrecks and high treason, of redemption and overcoming obstacles. There are so many wonderful works out there just waiting to be read, and this was the summer we would find them all.

"I'd like you to think about what books you want to read while you're out of school," I told them.

"*Calvin and Hobbes*," was my six-year-old's immediate reply.

One year on the way to our family vacation, the boys spent nearly eight hours reading *Calvin and Hobbes*. The four of them passed around six books, and I don't think they ever put those books down between home and our destination.

"Let's figure out something else," I suggested to my son that day. After seeing his horrified look, I quickly added, "in addition to *Calvin and Hobbes*." While I'm all for wild adventure and pithy one-liners, a little variety is always a good thing. A few years ago, I began to suspect there is such a thing as too much Calvin when I took the boys to get haircuts and seven-year-old Charlie asked the barber to make him look like Astro Boy.

Of course, the boys have read other books. But the truth is, *Calvin and Hobbes* is the standard to which all other great literature is held.

It's very tempting to just say yes, and welcome Calvin as son number six for the summer. When the boys are on a Calvin kick, I can count on hours of quiet as they sit and read and get high jinks inspiration. And there would be no shortage of reading materials since we own all the *Calvin and Hobbes* books. The boys have gotten these books on a variety of occasions including Christmas, birthdays, and as a reward for good behavior. That last category I find terribly ironic since Calvin sometimes inspires the very behavior we have worked to overcome.

It's not that Calvin gives them ideas they haven't already had—he simply stirs up a thought, a dream of a dream, and my boys are suddenly reminded of an outlandish rocket they'd like to build or how they'd love to get their hands on the baby doll of an unsuspecting neighbor girl—and catapult that doll to Planet Zorg.

They have never done that last thing, not yet anyway. Mostly, I think, because they do not have easy access to any doll collections.

They don't let that crush their hopes and dreams, however, and they are certainly inspired to do plenty else.

One afternoon I was busy with a project when Ethan, then nine, tapped me on the shoulder. I turned to find his entire face covered in Scotch tape. He was trying to get the tip of his nose to stick straight up, and he looked good. The minute I saw him, my mind flashed to a comic strip I cut out years ago of Calvin doing the very same thing. At the time, I was a college student who found the rascally behavior hilariously charming. I never would have predicted I'd have so many of my own Calvins, mimicking his antics.

If my boys declare Explosives as their college major, I'll have Calvin to thank.

Worse than nose taping and TNT, I'm afraid the boys look to Calvin when they think about girls. They often quote him when they talk of cooties and germs and the general ickiness these small females exude.

I'm all for my boys being immune to girlish charms—I'm going to enjoy it while it lasts. But we have to find a balance. One simply does not burp in a girl's face, I recently told one of the boys, no matter how much she claims to like it.

Many times, I must remind myself that our boys don't have a sister and thus lack at-home opportunities to learn about the female population. Being a former girl, I can tell the boys plenty, and I do my best to teach as we go. One afternoon the boys and I were taking a walk and enjoying the weather. One of the boys had gotten into trouble at school that day, saying something to the girl next to him that was rude and unacceptable. I was reminding my boys, all of them, that we as a family have standards for how we treat others.

"A gentleman," I explained, "doesn't treat other people that way."

"I," said one boy, "am no gentleman."

I assured my son he would be by the time his father and I were done with him.

And so, our work is cut out for us. Our job is to point their heads in the right direction. We will think lofty thoughts and talk of lofty things. We will discuss the great books. We will read of heroes who rescue others and overcome great obstacles. We will learn about men who make the right choices and find Truth along the way.

And then, once we're done with all that *Calvin and Hobbes*, we'll find some other cool stuff to read too.

The Sun Also Rises . . .
in Chuck Norris's Eyes

There are two kinds of people in this world: those who watch *Walker, Texas Ranger*, and those who do not.

Sadly for me, my family is part of the former. I'd add that this is unfortunate, but it's really only me who feels unfortunate about it. Every other member of my household thinks the sun rises and sets in Chuck Norris's eyes, that Law and Order (his right and left biceps) hold the answers to many of life's mysteries and dilemmas.

When my four older boys first started asking me about Chuck Norris several years ago, it was more as an urban legend, some kind of story they had heard from some source (I'm guessing their father) that they simply could not imagine. Kind of like the Loch Ness Monster, but with bigger quads.

"Who is this superhero," they would ask, "and can he really defeat bad guys just by looking at them?"

I was resistant to tell them about Chuck, I'll admit. They wanted to see him, to understand his ways. I thought not. I knew in my feminine gut that I would regret exposing my household of boys to Chuck Norris, with his weapons and explosions and roundhouse kicks to the face.

Of course, the other, bigger problem was that Chuck's

show, *Walker, Texas Ranger*, was in the television listings every single night of the week. In a fight versus the Texas Ranger, I knew who was going to lose.

And then one evening, as fate would have it, Daddy got home right around the time that I hit my wall. I was feeling tired, and *Walker, Texas Ranger* was on the TV. God smiled upon the Balducci boys. In a moment of weakness, I said yes to *Walker*. And there was no turning back.

I can't remember what episode was the first we ever saw. I bet if I asked one of the boys, he could tell me in detail. But as you can imagine, soon after that and despite my best efforts, *Walker* became a part of our evening rituals.

"Isn't *Nova* on PBS right now?" I'd ask some nights, trying to change things up, to get their minds off the Texas Ranger. But it was useless. For this season, things were set in stone. It became dinner, bath, prayers, and *Walker*. Always with a few spiraling crescent kicks along the way.

What is it about this show, I'd marvel, that makes it so irresistible to these boys? Sure there's the guaranteed two-explosion minimum, the fierce and menacing antagonists, the multiple car chases, and endless display of martial arts. But, I mean, really.

One late-summer afternoon, a thunderstorm rolled through, and I told the boys they could find something to watch on TV. I walked out of the room and came back a minute later to find all four of my sons in a trance.

I didn't know it then, but they were in what I now call a Walker Trance, so caught up in the glory of Chuck, of his beautiful roundhouse kicks and kung fu moves, that they were oblivious to the rest of the world. To snap them out of it, I tried to make a joke about Walker's extra-large belt buckle, but the boys barely looked in my direction. Who has time for jokes, they seemed to say, when Walker is right in the middle of serving up a heaping platter of Justice?

Soon after that, Walker confronted a bad guy by motioning to him with his pointer and middle fingers. Come here, beckoned the fingers, and let me show you how it's done.

Before I could laugh out loud at the unbelievable melodrama of it all, I glanced toward the boys to find each one of them silently mimicking Walker's move, daring the bad guy to mess with the four of them as well. Their eyes were fixed on the television, their fingers slowly bending in the air.

I called Paul a few minutes later to tell him about the scene, and his proud exhale let me know we wouldn't be turning the channel when he got home.

A Higher Power

One day we were discussing the birth of Jesus and how he left his grand home in heaven to come to earth. Instead of being a king in a grand castle, he spent his time on earth in a very humble environment.

"Why do you think the King of the entire universe came to earth and was born in a stable?" I asked them.

"To show he could take it," said one of the boys, "kinda like Chuck Norris."

It can sometimes be quite a challenge to delve into spirituality with my sons. For so long, my notions concerning religious matters centered on a "God is Love and Love is Tranquil" mentality, an idea that godliness was a gentle, breeze-in-your-hair, speak-in-a-whisper way of behaving.

That this is not my personality at all presented a wide variety of problems, mainly that I spent years berating myself for not being a quiet and gentle soul who acted saintly and good.

"Stop talking so loud," I would chide myself. "A holy woman should be quieter than this."

And lo and behold I wound up with a houseful of boys who are even more rambunctious than I could ever be.

Fortunately for me, before my boys started coming of age, I began to embrace the idea of God-given personalities. I started to accept that a big part of my makeup as a human being was simply who God made me to be. That's not to say we don't all need plenty of refining, but I finally realized that history is filled with good men and women who loved God but who were more than whispering souls floating their way through this earthly life and on into the next.

My boys have a notion that God is like Chuck Norris, and as long as they remember it's God first, Chuck second, I don't really have a problem with that. Faith will appeal to them if they see God as someone they can identify with—a strong man who wants to protect and defend those he loves.

There is still plenty of tweaking to be done in the midst of this journey. God is certainly powerful and strong, but he doesn't drive around heaven in an army tank.

Or does he?

History 101

It is after dinner. Homework is done, boys are bathed, and we have some time before bed. In moments like these, we turn to our dear friend Chuck.

We are watching *Walker, Texas Ranger*. One of the boys comments that a particular character is Chuck Norris's brother.

"No," I tell him, "they aren't brothers."

"But it said his name was Aaron Norris," the boys protest.

"Oh," I say, "I think that's his son."

"Are you sure that isn't his brother?" asks my husband.

"Wait," says another boy, "didn't Chuck change his name?"

"That's right," I realize, "his name was Carlos Rey."

And then it occurs to me, with some shock and awe, that we have just discussed the personal life of Chuck Norris as if he is a dear family friend. Which, on more than a few days, I feel like he is.

One summer afternoon, we brought a friend with us to the pool. On the drive, the boys started discussing heritage and ethnic roots.

"We're part German," offered the friend.

"Well, we," said six-year-old Augie with a sigh, "are part Chuck Norris."

Birthday Parties for Boys

One afternoon I overheard the boys discussing birthday parties. We had recently celebrated Elliott's tenth birthday, and everyone was still pumped about how much fun it had been.

For Elliott's party that year, we had hosted friends and cousins and celebrated with a Sports Party.

The schedule went something like this:

1. Guests arrive.
2. Everyone plays basketball in the driveway.
3. Feed everyone dinner of Elliott's favorite foods: hot dogs, Doritos, Dr Pepper.
4. Everyone plays soccer in the backyard.
5. Feed everyone cake.
6. Everyone plays touch football in the backyard.
7. Open gifts.
8. Send everyone home.

That party was every bit as simple as it looks on paper—but it was also a blast. The boys had a wonderful time, and they were still talking about it days later.

"For my next party, I'm going to do something like that," said one of the boys, "and at the end of the night, we're gonna tell facts about Chuck Norris."

Chuck Norris trivia. The only thing that could have made that party better.

Another standout party in our Boy Party History was one we hosted for Ethan's eighth birthday. My husband had just finished reading *Treasure Island* to our boys, and our household was on a pirate kick.

Ethan invited the boys in his class at school. After a few classic party games (relay races, determine what items are in this sock), I told the boys we were going to be treated to a special guest. The guest, I explained, was going to ask us a few questions about a literary passage I was going to read to everyone.

I pulled out *Treasure Island* and told the boys we'd listen to one chapter, and I was pleasantly surprised by the general lack of eye rolling. The boys sat relatively quiet and listened to the tale.

A few minutes later, out came Pirate Paul (who looked remarkably like my husband in a wig). Pirate Paul had long black tresses that were lovingly braided, as well as a gold hoop earring and a wicked pirate accent.

"Aaarrgh," he bellowed. "Where's me birthday boy?"

For those reeling from Paul's willingness to dress up, this is where I should mention that I almost didn't get Pirate Paul to attend our party. That morning, just as I finished pulling together the costume, my husband started to buck. He wasn't too sure about making an absolute fool of himself in front of a bunch of eight-year-old boys (and other grown-up guests). He left for work unconvinced of any special guest appearances that evening.

But on the way to the office, my husband heard one of his favorite radio hosts talking about a similar experience he had, how he did something silly for his own son and how it was absolutely worth it.

Paul came home that afternoon ready for the party. He

dressed up and looked ridiculous—and the look on Ethan's face when his father came into the front room dressed as a pirate made it absolutely worth it. I happened to take a picture at that very moment, and it is a picture I treasure. The smile on our son's face is something I will never forget.

That moment also made me somehow love my husband even more.

Only once have we spent an inordinate amount of money on a birthday party. It was the summer baby Henry was born, and the summer felt like a bit of a bust. New babies are wonderful, but they can sure cramp your style. The boys didn't complain—they were more than willing to watch those countless hours of television. But I wanted to go out with a bang, to have a proper send-off to a summer that had sort of dragged on just a bit.

We combined two of the boys' birthdays and invited all their friends plus a few more, all the cousins, and even a few of my own friends and neighbors. For four hours, we rented an inflatable waterslide that took up almost our entire backyard. It was huge and impressive and very, very wet.

As each guest walked into the yard and saw the enormous slide, he would shriek with delight. Over and over, guests rode down the slide, which was pretty much the extent of the party. I could barely get those boys to eat or sing or do anything remotely birthday partyish beyond just having fun. After two hours, everyone left, and my boys and husband spent the other two hours taking advantage of having the slide to themselves. Paul continued to ride until the owner came to retrieve his slide, and even then he had to practically beg my husband to stop riding because it was getting late and he needed to leave.

SINGLE-GENDER SIBLING LIVING

Advantages

1. If you don't like your Christmas gifts, trade with a brother.
2. You like his shirt? It's yours in twelve to eighteen months.
3. None of that pesky modesty to deal with.
4. Retaliation for ALL.
5. Hannah Who?
6. When shopping with Mom, no need to stop in the pink aisle.
7. Most likely never own a sissy dog (or a kitty).
8. No one gets scared when we watch Lord of the Rings.
9. Tree fort guaranteed cootie-free.

Disadvantages

1. Mom tries enforcing hand-me-down undies. Thank goodness for Dad.

5

Keeping Up
Appearances

Elements of Style

When in public, how good I look is directly proportional to how bad the boys look. This is how I cope.

It is an evening in fall, and our family is walking out the door to attend a neighborhood potluck. Elliott is wearing his basketball shorts—the ones he wears all the time, the ones I have to sneak into the wash every third day so they don't stand up on their own and threaten to picket. He has paired these gray and white shorts with a green T-shirt that is unraveling at the sleeve. He is also wearing his running shoes (which are relatively new, so a few points for me!) and his black school socks that come midway between his ankle and his shin.

He is a vision of classiness.

"Honey," I call to my husband, "how do you feel about the way this boy is dressed?"

"He looks great," says my husband.

I head to the bathroom to add another coat of lipstick. And also some pearls.

My theory is this: the more presentable I am, the less presentable my boys need to be. Or maybe it's the less presentable my boys are, the better I need to look. Either way, I understand this totally flies in the face of reason and common sense, but most days it's all I've got.

My husband, who has since learned the art of looking presentable in public, was once this same creature. Like his boys, he slept in his clothes for the next day, clothes that were also conveniently what he already had on. Isn't life great!

Paul now puts on fresh, decent-looking clothes each and every day. As an attorney, he may have gone to the other extreme. I sometimes suspect he would sleep in a tie if he knew it wouldn't wrinkle. So I have hope that a hypoallergenic sense of fashion will kick in with my boys as well. I cling to this hope. For now I have to rely on the family rule that certain formal occasions are nonnegotiable; I do that and then pray I have really good hair days the rest of the time.

Not that my boys totally appreciate my efforts.

One evening I was getting ready for a date with Paul. I had applied a little more makeup than normal in celebration of eating at an establishment that didn't serve ketchup in packets. In that vein, I was also wearing a colorful new sweater and some sparkly, dangly earrings.

"How do I look?" I asked Charlie. I noticed that he was staring at me, and I wondered if he was swept away by my beauty.

"You look like a gypsy," he answered.

"Um, is that good or bad?" I asked.

"It's good," he assured me. "Gypsies are awesome. They've got, like, guitars and guns and stuff like that."

Traveling with Boys

One year Paul and I took the boys on a whirlwind end-of-summer vacation, a last-minute trip that included stops in Atlanta, Emmitsburg, Gettysburg, and Washington, D.C.

People reported hearing the sounds of wailing, which could have been my voice echoing down the Blue Ridge Parkway and into your home. Driving through seven states with five boys in one day can do that to a woman.

The trip was actually quite fun, filled with high adventure and minimal tears (from me or anyone else). Our boys have always been good travelers—armed with *Calvin and Hobbes*, they can ride for hours. However, I have to remind myself that for boys, every hour spent in the car being good requires seven minutes of frantic jumping on the hotel beds when we arrive at our destination. I'm not saying I encourage that kind of behavior; that's just how long I have to work to nip that behavior in the bud.

I had wanted to take my boys on this trip for a while, to travel up to our nation's capital and show them some of our incredibly rich history. I realized a few months ago that this summer would be a good time to make the effort. The next year, Henry would be a toddler and perhaps not as agreeable when it comes to extended time in the car and also in public.

During our time in D.C., we stopped at multiple monuments and historic buildings, and also took several hours to visit a few Smithsonian Museums. While I would have enjoyed time at the National Portrait Gallery and the Freer Gallery of Art, Paul and I realized that the boys would most enjoy the buildings filled with rockets and weapons and large, taxidermed animals. We were correct.

When I asked the boys what their favorite part of that day was, they were quick to mention dinosaur skeletons and airplanes. They seemed especially enamored with the many airplanes on display at the Air and Space Museum (always my favorite growing up), as well as the chance to maneuver an airplane control panel.

On another day, we stopped in Emmitsburg, Maryland, home to both the National Shrine Grotto of Lourdes and Mount St. Mary's Seminary, where our friend and former pastor is now working.

When I was in high school, my family visited the Grotto, and I have always remembered that stop with fondness. A friend recently described the Grotto as being "spiritually infused," and I think that description is perfect—even as a teenager I felt an incredible peace and closeness to God during our hours there.

Visiting the seminary was a highlight of the trip, and we especially enjoyed spending time with our priest friend. Everything about this campus appeals to the nature of boys, including the endless hiking trails, large open fields surrounded by steep hills, and a cafeteria with every food imaginable. (The boys wanted to stay for lunch as the pizza bar would then be open.) It was a perfect day.

Throughout our trip, we had stops at the Atlanta Zoo and the battlefields at Gettysburg, and spent an evening with my cousin (he who has a television the size of my Suburban). We also spent the night on the campus of the nation's oldest school for the deaf, which I recommend when traveling with a bunch of boys. We drove home through the mountains and saw groups of deer staring at us in the mist. All in all, a just-right trip for boys.

It is easy sometimes to fixate on what a vacation with boys is not—it isn't quiet or calm or terribly relaxing. But it is fun—it's my life, and it's quite an adventure.

It's All Greek

There is an almost-empty two-liter soda bottle in the fridge, a remnant of a recent birthday party that featured all of ten-year-old Elliott's favorite foods—hot dogs, Doritos, and his favorite bubbly, Dr Pepper. The birthday boy pulls out the bottle and beckons his brothers into the dining room.

"Who wants to see me chug it?" Elliott shouts.

They begin to chant.

"Chug it! Chug it!"

Elliott throws back the bottle and downs the rest of the soda.

Baby Henry is worn out from the party and goes to bed easily. A few hours later, I enter his room to find he has thrown up everywhere, large chunks of last night's buffet strewn across the crib.

I walk into the front room where the boys are watching television. I notice that our large Persian rug is folded almost completely in half. I look closer to see that six-year-old Augie is rolled up inside it.

"What are you doing?" I ask.

He explains that he was cold and didn't want to get up to fetch a blanket.

Some days, I tell my husband, my life really is like living in a frat house.

Work Ethic

I wish my boys woke up every morning clamoring to keep this house in order, ready to take on the day by first doing a deep clean of our environs. Sadly, they do not. If left to their own devices, they would spend hours watching television, flipping between the big game and Animal Planet's *When Sharks Attack*.

But this is our home, not a frat house. So clean we must.

Despite the initial moans and groans, the boys will get the job done, because once I put my mind to it, I can get them to do anything. My personal goal is to have them working with happy hearts by the time they are twenty-four. I think that's mostly realistic. I also think it will earn major points from whatever women my sons choose to marry.

Once my boys get going on housework, they generally get excited about it. The challenge is getting over that initial knee-jerk reaction. "What?" I'll hear them moan. "It's time to clean AGAIN? We just did that last week!"

Some days I'm tempted to point out that they change their underwear and brush their teeth on a daily basis too, despite the fact that they'll just have to do it again, the very next day. But I fear this analogy might inspire them in the totally wrong direction. "You're right," I'm afraid I'll hear, "let's never change our underwear again!"

One Saturday morning, it was time for chores, and I gave

each boy an option between two things. "Pick which job you want," I told them, "and then do it."

Eight-year-old Charlie decided he would clean a bathroom, and off he went to get his supplies. He put on the gloves and I helped him pour the pine cleaner into the toilet. I always help with this step, because one of the boys once used an entire bottle of cleaner to wipe down the toilet in the boys' bathroom. This approach did wonders for the room's aroma, but that route could get pricey.

I gave the toilet a generous but reasonable dose of cleanser, and then left my son to his chores.

Fifteen minutes later, he came to me, done with his work.

"That was great," he exclaimed. "When I grow up, I want to do that for a living."

"You want to clean bathrooms for a living?" I asked him.

"Yep," he said, "I'm going to be a plumber."

"A plumber doesn't clean bathrooms," said my husband, walking into the room. "What you want is to be a *janitor*."

As he said these words, my husband got a faraway look in his eyes, a dreamy sound in his voice. In college, Paul and his best friend had part-time jobs cleaning commercial buildings. Those days as a janitor, says Paul, were some of the happiest of his life.

"Yes," said Charlie that morning, more convinced than ever, "I'm going to be a *janitor*."

But while this particular boy plans on cleaning for a living, it seems he's not motivated to clean in his own home, beyond that brief interlude with cleaning a toilet.

One summer morning I announced to the boys it was time to do a few chores.

"Boys," I began, and before I could even finish my sentence, Elliott had thrown back his head, let out a heavy sigh, and wriggled up his nose.

I let out a deep sigh too, desperately wanting to be a patient person, desperately wishing I was not given so many opportunities to achieve that goal.

"Son," I said, "what are you going to do when you get older and live in your own house? How do you think it's going to stay clean?"

His younger brother, the future janitor, had the easy answer.

"We're going to hire a maid."

A boy's life in a three-word chapter: "I'm bleeding again."

Cultural Awareness

"How do you say 'waffles' in French?" asks Augie. "Isn't it *vaffles*?

Boys are capable of good behavior. It's important you don't forget that. I have gone through seasons where I've lowered my standards because that seems like a healthy alternative to going bald from pulling out my hair. But then, after a few weeks of letting my sons act like pint-sized bohemians, I wake up and realize they are better than this, that we as a family are better than this. That's when I snap to and decide I'm ready to welcome back my great expectations.

I've seen my sons rise to the occasion. I know it can be done. The trick is to remember that there is a time and a place for everything. I want well-behaved sons; I think the universe would appreciate that from me. But I realize (now, after a few years of painful trial-and-error) that their best efforts will not always meet my standards, and that sometimes—but not always—my standards need to be adjusted.

The key is to keep having standards. Never let them take that away from you.

Ultimately, no matter what craziness my boys throw my way, I will not relinquish my ideals, my desire to do the best we can, even on the days when that's a painfully relative ideal. Some days, having standards might simply mean no one burps their ABCs (at the table) and remembering my furniture is not a trampoline. Sometimes, the standards are much higher and require appropriate public behavior and possibly wearing a tie.

My key to attaining success with standards is telling the boys up front what is expected of them, and to then apprise them of what will happen if they don't tow the line.

It's probably not fair of me to just set that before you and leave you thinking this is entirely effective. Boys are generally not motivated by a sense of propriety. They are not typically built to please authority.

Oh sure, you can say you will be "disappointed" if they have a competition to see who can spit the farthest off the hotel balcony, but don't be shocked if that doesn't stop the spitting. Saying it will make baby Jesus cry if they arm wrestle in church isn't all that compelling either. I have tried this more subtle approach, and in the end, I've found the most effective method to be the one called Don't Do It Or Else. And then clearly define Or Else.

Having said that, boys are absolutely capable of rising to the occasion. They can behave and do what is right, and when that happens you will be so proud of their efforts, it will keep you going through the next dry spell until you experience success again.

A few weeks after Henry was born, we decided to take the boys on a last-minute end-of-summer trip. We had been cooped up in the house because the oppressive heat prevented a lot of outdoor time with a newborn baby. I was feeling stir-crazy and guilty, worried that the boys would look back on this summer as a bust.

My husband had business in another city, and I booked a room at a nice hotel that was near his meetings. We decided the trip would include a day at the newly opened aquarium and a fun evening at this posh hotel. The posh part was more for me, but since the booking rate included aquarium tickets—and I didn't plan on leaving the room once we checked in—after that, I was sold.

At the end of a long day of looking at fish and whales and every other sea creature imaginable, we headed to our hotel to clean up (and jump on the beds) and grab dinner. We had hoped to eat on the way to the hotel, but never saw anything. After further research, we discovered that the only restaurant open was the five-star steakhouse attached to the hotel. As we stood in the lobby, Paul and I looked over at the glass-walled eatery. Towering chandeliers glistened in the distance, giving a soft glow to the expansive wine collection on prominent display.

"No way," I told my husband. That was all I could muster.

"At this point, it's our only option," my husband said, and I made him promise that he'd stand by me if our children were responsible for that myriad of bottles winding up on the floor.

This is where I should point out that need for a balance in expectations. It's not that I would ever knowingly let my boys touch those bottles. I had no plans for them to get within reading distance of them. But the thing is: you never know.

Just by stepping through those enormous, heavy glass doors, I was opening us up to the possibility that somehow, in a moment of sheer dumb luck, one boy might manage to break free or reach out or even just breathe hard enough to somehow knock over those bottles and destroy the entire shimmery scene.

What's the lesson to be learned here? I'm not sure. Because on the one hand, I realize that at some point, a boy becomes a young man who will eventually have to enter such a restaurant if he wants to wine and dine a lady. But when is that point, and how will you know?

That evening in the restaurant ended up being perfect. It was a turning point for us because it was the first time we'd done any fine dining as a family (unless you count our local Mexican restaurant), and we had a positive, beautiful experience. I wasn't rushing out to take a vacation at an upscale resort after that, but at least we now recognized that we had more options—options that didn't include paper cups and supersized fries.

Sometimes, with all these standards and expectations and finding the balance between high hopes and reality, you have to take risks—and that's where you have the chance to succeed.

FAMILY RULES, WRITTEN AND UNWRITTEN

We have rules around this house, a list of standards that we enforce and observe. It's a way of training our boys to show grace and courtesy to those around them and also to keep me from graying prematurely.

I was inspired to make this list after reading a practical book on parenting. The list hangs in our kitchen, and when I'm feeling low on energy and patience, I simply point to the standard or rule being broken before following through with consequences.

Our Standards and Rules:

- We do not engage in name-calling or put-downs.
- We do not interrupt; we wait to talk.
- We respect each other's privacy and personal property. We knock before entering a closed room, get permission before borrowing.
- If we accidentally make a mess, we clean it up.
- No unauthorized eating between meals. Ask Mom!
- All clothing is either on us, in drawers, or in the hamper.
- We make our own beds in the morning.
- We fulfill our "house responsibilities" (our chores) promptly and to the best of our ability. This includes assignments for school.
- We devote most of family life to healthy work and play, not glued to the tube. We spend our time in conversation, reading, study, chores, and games—getting to know and appreciate each other in the few precious years we have together as a family.

Beyond this practical life list, there is another spectrum we are forced to cover. I'm amazed at the things I need to spell out to my boys, discussions about behavior that involves them doing things I would have never dreamed up. As boys, I suspect, they think up new realms of stuff to stay occupied and also drive me batty. I wonder if they labor under the burden that it's their responsibility to make sure I don't get bored or complacent.

When it comes to outlandish behavior, it does not always occur to me what I should forewarn or ban. It was not "against the rules" for my boys to climb on the roof of the concession stand at the pool because I never could have predicted they'd actually do it. Imagine my surprise and embarrassment when my friend informed me that my son had done just that, when she was watching my boys at the pool. "Thanks," I said, "I'll be sure and add that to our list of unacceptable behavior."

In the rare event that I actually think of some bit of outlandish behavior first, I am learning to discuss it right away. In the past, I wouldn't bother to talk about thoughts I'd have, visions if you will, of some random form of badness that might be possible to perform, because really, who would do such a thing?

The answer, I now know: boys.

Whatever crazy idea I can hatch, my boys can hatch it better. If I ever have an inkling of a thought of some form of wild behavior—tying the skateboard to the back of the car to catch a ride, for instance—then I'd better just talk about it now so we can nip it in the bud.

"Boys," I said one afternoon, "you know that if you ever tried jumping off the roof of the garage while holding onto a plastic bag—you realize that won't work, right?"

Silence for a moment, and then nods.

"But why not?" one ventured.

And then I'm absolutely glad I broached the subject.

Some days, I will hear someone say off in the distance something like, "I tried that once and nearly broke my neck," or "Is it true that someone can run so fast they can run on the ceiling?" And then someone answers no, not on the ceiling, but they can run up walls. That's my cue to enter scene.

So in addition to our published list of standards, we have another list longer and more encompassing. It is an ever-blossoming list, the nonpublished Things We Just Don't Do. This list has become my life's work. Nearly every day there is some new, insanely over-the-top behavior the boys try out that I then must add to the list.

The current list is based on past actions as well as my imagination, and it includes things like:

- no beating the tops of trucks with bats;
- just stay off the tops of all cars in general;
- don't get on the roof either;
- that includes Gramma and Papa's roof next door;
- no throwing things out of second-story windows;

Keeping Up Appearances

- yes, even if you have a bucket below to catch them;
- especially not Daddy's underwear and our nicely bound books;
- no eating without permission;
- no cooking without permission;
- no starting fires without permission;
- even if you have dug a large hole in the backyard and you are confident it would be perfectly safe to have a bonfire, this is absolutely OFF LIMITS;
- if you break any of these rules, pray you have large and attentive guardian angels who look like Chuck Norris and act like him too.

6

Essentials
of a Boy's Life

LEGO Madness

One evening, at the end of a long day, I realized I was walking with a limp. I had been down on the floor for over an hour, working alongside ten-year-old Elliott as we toiled over LEGO pieces.

I found myself amazed at how well my boy could maneuver these tiny bits of plastic. I was equally amazed at my inability to successfully press together two miniscule plastic bricks. I would clumsily press and destroy while my son would somehow produce creation after stunning creation.

I am not normally a LEGO-building mom. While I love these classic building blocks, I tend to be more of an admirer from afar. I ooh and aah when the boys show me their architectural designs, but I'm comfortable to leave it at that. They are the team, and I am their cheerleader.

On that particular evening, in the moments before I hobbled around the house, I had been acting out of the ordinary. It was not my first choice, or even my second—but I owed it to this child.

That evening, I sat and helped create, but it was not just an act of kindness—it was an act of reparation.

A few weeks earlier, Elliott wanted one thing for his upcoming birthday—a set of LEGOs so large and vast that they practically needed a crane to get it off the shelf at the toy store.

"Am I really about to buy another thousand pieces of

LEGOs?" I asked myself as I stood in the building blocks aisle. "And how can there be a thousand pieces of LEGOs that we don't already own?"

But of course, we don't have anywhere near all the LEGOs available for purchase because they make new ones every single day.

When Elliott opened his gift on the afternoon of his birthday, this boy started to jump up and down. He then grabbed the brother nearest to him and those two started jumping. Eventually a third brother joined in, and the three of them fell to the ground in a giant heap of LEGO-induced euphoria.

Over the next few days, the boys all huddled in the playroom working on this castle that, when it was finished, might possibly be large enough to hold their baby brother—they were still eyeing its structural soundness to be sure. For hours they labored, making piles and working individually and then as a team. It was beautiful, and the sight of those boys working so hard in such unity for so long made it worth every single one of those many, many pennies we spent on that LEGO castle.

Finally, the castle was finished. The boys called me into the room and had a grand unveiling that included me shrieking with delight and the four of them humbly accepting my praise. They were terribly pleased with themselves.

And then, two days later, I destroyed the castle.

I was cleaning the playroom to get ready for company, and I needed to move the LEGOs upstairs.

"Don't move the castle," my boys pleaded and begged. "It will fall apart."

"It won't fall apart," I assured them. "I will be very careful."

I went on to explain that I would take great pains to get the castle safely up the stairs for a thousand more hours of fun.

"I am a grown-up," I told the boys. "I know how to properly handle your toys."

But of course they were right. I had slowly carried the castle of a thousand pieces the entire journey, and just as I lowered it toward its new location, it splintered and split and splayed across the bedroom floor. I thought I was going to pass out. I wanted to die.

When my boys came home from school that afternoon, they were understandably devastated. The birthday boy in particular had a remarkably long period of mourning, a very loud and drawn-out time of grieving.

"Why?" he asked. "WWWHHYYYY????"

"It was an accident," I explained, trying to stay calm. I had decided, the minute this horror occurred, that if I got too worked up, it would only fuel the fire.

"Why did you do this?" Elliott asked again, and again I explained that I never meant to hurt him. It was beginning to sound like a breakup.

My boy, while understandably upset, was going on a bit long. I told him (in continued forced calm) that while I understood how sad he was, he could not carry on in that manner anywhere but in his room. So off he went, where he closed the door and continued to grieve in such a manner that the entire rest of the house could hear. If those walls could talk, I decided, they would ask him to be quiet.

After a while, I went up to see him.

"I understand you are upset," I said with control, "but this is going on a little long, don't you think?"

No, as a matter of fact, he did not.

I left the room, and a while later Elliott emerged. He was nearly dehydrated from all the sadness, the unbearable grief of losing something so precious as this castle.

My son came to my side and gave me a long, tight hug.

"I forgive you, Mom," he said. He wanted to know exactly how I felt about my horrible deed. "What did you do when you dropped the castle?"

"I cried," I said. And that was the truth—when I realized what I had done, and all the sadness it was going to cause, I did cry, just a little. Maybe it was tears of frustration, but probably I cried because I knew that split-second error was going to cost me. A lot.

A few days after that, as I hobbled around the house, I realized that it had.

I had spent a chunk of that evening curled up on the floor, my legs entwined like a human pretzel. I sat with my boy, and we looked for tiny gray pieces while I fervently begged God to help us get this puzzle together again.

That evening, as I watched my son deftly handle this renovation, I realized that I sometimes underestimate my boys.

It's true I could give them a stick and they would play outside for hours—they are certainly drawn to the simple beauty of creation and adventure.

But building a three-story siege tower is a lot harder than it looks. At the end of a long evening, I realized that it takes real finesse to play with Legos. When boys huddle around these building developments, they are doing real work—real work that I have now learned to avoid handling at all costs.

Books of the Highest Quality

We love the library. When we go, the books we get focus mainly on animals, sports, and sports involving animals. Sometimes we break out and look at books about competition, about the history of competition and how to win.

One afternoon we came across a recent edition of the *Guinness Book of World Records*. The oldest boy was the first to get his hands on the book, and he read it the entire way home and then most of the afternoon.

Every so often, Ethan would come find me.

"Did you know," he said, "that Evel Knievel once broke every single bone in his body?"

He seemed a little too enamored with this idea, and I felt compelled to highlight all the reasons breaking a lot of bones would not be a good idea. It might get you in the *Guinness Book*, I said, but that is where the victories would end.

Over the course of our time with this book, my sons learned about the man who had the longest nose hair (interesting), the couple who kissed the longest (gross), and the person who had produced the burp with the highest decibel count (awesome). The boys had a serious discussion about the record holder who threw a bottle cap the farthest, and they felt this record was something that with a bit of effort they might possibly challenge.

Pretty soon, every feat and deed held the potential of

getting into The Book. Every action was assessed for its speed and height and degree of danger. If it didn't require freakish body parts or living in Nepal, the boys considered it doable.

"How fast do you think I could go down that hill?" I'd overhear. "How tall could we build a tower of blocks?" They wondered about jumping high and growing tall and riding fast while on a bike tied to the back of the car.

I'm all for a healthy challenge, but of course I was obligated to crush their dreams if the dreams were going to send us to the emergency room. When they pored over ways to invent the first dependable jet pack, it made me nervous. "Why don't you try building the longest working straw?" I'd suggest. "Okay," they'd answer, "right after we figure out where we'll store the pack's extra fuel."

The same trip to the library that led to the *Guinness Book* also opened the door to another incredible discovery, a book that the boys discussed with equal fervor.

While we were at the library that day, as the boys huddled around *Guinness*, I set out to find some other books to bring home. Perhaps they'll need a break from the records, I thought, and went to the animal section for some of the regulars and maybe something new too.

There, in the Ocean and Sea Life section, I found a large, brightly colored book about ocean animals featuring stunning, page-sized photographs.

I chose the book because the layout was clean and the pictures were very big. Each page featured two or three photographs of dolphins and whales, a look at their life in the ocean as they swam and ate and interacted with others. It was lovely.

The book was quite popular with the boys, but after a few days I started to notice it was often lying open on the same page. I would find the book on the coffee table or the floor in the study or up in the boys' bedrooms, and nearly every time with this particular page showing.

One day, Charlie brought the book to me.

"You've got to see this," he said, putting the book in my lap. It was on the same page it always seemed to be, and there I saw a very large flesh-colored object protruding from a whale.

"What is this?" I asked him.

"'Pictured at left . . . ,'" he began, and he went on to read that the image was the very large reproductive organ of a male grey whale.

My jaw dropped.

"Isn't that awesome?" said Charlie, looking at me. "I think it's as big as our Suburban."

Most-Favored Toy

When our oldest son was a baby, I remember talking to Paul's sister about toys for boys.

"You will be amazed at what boys like to play with," she told me.

My sister-in-law has three children, a boy in between two girls. She was always intrigued that the boy would make his own suitable toys if none were available.

"This boy," she said of her son, "will take a pretzel stick in each hand and use them as a pair of guns."

I thought that was pretty creative, but I assumed he did that because he already had a plastic gun from which to garner inspiration. My son, I had decided, would have no such thing.

When I was growing up, my brothers were not allowed to have weapons. We never had plastic swords or knives, and certainly no guns of any kind. I never knew this was exceptional, and I was mostly so caught up in bossing around my younger siblings that I didn't realize my parents were working to deliberately avoid these kinds of toys. All I knew is that I could get my brothers to play school and house, and even dentist, and I loved them for it.

When my boys started looking for toys, I saw a definite attraction to weapons. We didn't have any pretend guns in our home, but when playing with friends who did, weapons were always the first toys of choice.

Despite their being drawn to guns and swords, I still wouldn't buy any—but I began to notice a trend. The Tinkertoys became guns. Sticks became guns. Even a half-eaten grilled cheese sandwich was somehow a very good gun.

Guns, as my boys saw it, were everywhere.

Years later, when I threw in the towel on weapons-free living, I asked my mom how she did it.

"How did you raise five boys who never played with weapons?" I asked.

They played with weapons all the time, my mom told me. They just made them out of sticks and blocks and anything else they could get their hands on.

This explains that strange phenomenon of how a home can be devoid of weapons and somehow filled with them at the very same time.

"When I go to college," declared Elliott, "I won't only study about sports. I'm also going to spend some time studying dynamite."

Good Stuff

"Is this anybody's?" asks my husband, pulling out a large PVC concoction from under the deck.

"No way," I say, eyeing the piece with disdain. Who would want an old, warped concoction of plastic pipes? Why on earth would we hold onto such a thing? It is junk. I ponder all these issues, and just before I tell my husband to ditch the rickety object, two of the boys claim it at the same time.

"Yes," they shout in unison, "it's mine!"

Our garage is filled with many questionable items. Whenever we head out there as a family to clean up the area, Paul and I wind up having a "difference of opinion." I am inclined to just throw everything away. He wants to keep it all.

When will we ever need a set of half-broken croquet mallets, I ask him. He's not sure, but he doesn't want to risk being without. Okay, I say, moving right along, let's at least get rid of this old bow-and-arrow target, and these deflated soccer balls. No can do, says my husband, those could come in handy.

I heave a sigh of frustration. I want a garage that looks like the ones I see on television—the kind that have actual cars parked in them. Instead, we are Sanford and Son for pint-sized warriors.

What I have learned is the art of sitting back, of trying to chill out and release that area to my husband. It's out of my domain, I tell myself, let it go. If I can't get rid of any of the junk, then I won't look at my garage with the eyes of what it could be. One day, it will be clean. One day, I might even show it to my friends.

Until then, it belongs to the men. And every so often, when I'm feeling like the time might be right to purge, I will happen upon a sight to keep me in my place. I will look out the kitchen window to find an arsenal, a fort filled with bandits armed with croquet mallets, the walls of the fort reinforced by old bow-and-arrow targets, the encroaching bad guys being pummeled by deflated soccer balls.

Leisurely Pastimes

Life outdoors is simple and fun.

When the boys are not making forts and attacking imaginary bad guys, they are working on their basketball skills or their golf swing. If they aren't focused on combat or sports, then there is only one other thing on their minds: fire.

My boys love fire. We have spent countless days—days, not hours—in the backyard by our fire pit. Paul will take an entire afternoon to burn old wood and chop kindling, while the boys gather sticks to throw in the fire.

It's all very monitored, and we proceed with forced caution. Being careful is certainly an acquired skill, and we are trying to instill this trait in our children. It's taking some effort.

What it all comes down to is this: burning stuff is fun. It doesn't matter what it is—if Daddy says yes, into the fire it goes.

I can't say any of this surprises me. This condition of pyromania is actually one of the few things they got from me. Not that I'm proud of it or anything, but it's been handy to have a few stories in my repertoire that involve me and small fires that turned into a big deal. Those tales have gotten a lot of mileage around here, and hopefully they have made an impression.

None of this, ultimately, will diminish my boys' love of

fire. They will spend as much time stoking a fire as we have to offer, whether it's the brief flicker of a candle or hours by a bonfire.

One Thanksgiving the boys spent half the day tending flames. After our main meal, Paul and the boys headed out to the backyard and got to work on something nice in the firepit. After a while, my husband let each of the boys start their own mini-fire in a separate but nearby section of the yard.

And I wonder why I have no grass. In order to safely do this, there needed to be plenty of dirt, and that is now what fills my yard—miniature sandtraps for miniature pyros.

The boys split into two groups of two, each team working furiously to get a blaze better than the other. Competition is indeed our middle name, and when it speaks, these boys listen.

After a while, Team II had produced a raging fire (relatively speaking), and those two boys decided to invite their brothers to come enjoy the glow.

"This fire is dominant," beckoned one boy. "You'd better just come stand by ours."

Cow Boy

Years ago, when our son Charlie was three, he developed an intense fascination with cows. In the way many boys become obsessed with dinosaurs, Charlie wanted to know everything about cows.

Around that time, we started checking out all the cow books at the library. We began researching different kinds of cows, what cows did for fun, where they lived, and what they liked to eat. We would slow down whenever we passed a field of cows, and when the rodeo came to town, we made sure to stop by and visit all the steer.

The high point of this season came when Charlie started begging to have a cow come live with us. That and the constant presence of Carlito, an imaginary cow who for a short time became Charlie's best friend. "Don't sit there," my toddler would order. "Carlito is there."

For his fourth birthday, Charlie had a cow party. Not a cowboy party. Just a cow party. His cake had a gigantic black-and-white cow fashioned out of the most delicious butter-cream frosting (the hot pink udder was scrumptious). His gifts included a plush cow, a board game about cows, and a popular children's book that featured cows who could type.

Over time, Charlie's obsession with cows began to wane, and he began to focus on more typical boyhood themes—dinosaurs and spaceships and sports. But it was clear there would always be a place in his heart for the beloved bovine.

One night at dinner, not long after his cow phase had ended, I caught my son pulling pepperonis off his pizza and casually tossing them on the floor.

"Pick that up," I said. "We don't live in a barn!"

"Yes, ma'am," he said wistfully, "but I sure wish we did."

Games We Play

Everything is quiet. Charlie is standing at the dining room table finishing a small bowl of ice cream. Ethan is heading off to get ready for bed. Augie is standing on the living room couch, examining his teeth in the nearby mirror on the wall.

Suddenly, Elliott bursts from the closet under the stairs. He flings open the door and races through the dining room, his feet and arms flailing as he sprints for something in the front room.

"Safe!" he yells. "I'm safe!" Everyone looks in his direction, and there is surprise on each face. It slowly dawns on the other boys where their brother has been, that he had never been caught in their game of hide-and-seek, the one that ended about ten minutes earlier.

Games are loud in my house. The reason I will never get rid of the television is that when I allow the boys to watch, it's the one time I'm guaranteed a little quiet. Yes, I'm using the TV to sedate my children. If you saw how wild things can get, you would not judge me.

Even reading time is somehow less quiet than I once imagined. My boys do love to read, but often they find their books a little too inspiring. One minute they are curled on the couch, reading the adventures of river-raft cruises or epic battles between men and orcs. The next thing I know, they are drawing up plans to build their own river raft and are staging their own epic battle that pits brother against brother. Acting out these battles is not nearly as tranquil as reading about them.

Board games become action packed too. One night, I rounded up the boys for a game of Yahtzee. This game is a personal favorite of mine, and the boys are all now at good ages to play. Henry was in bed, and I was looking forward to a calm evening of rolling dice and keeping quiet, gentle tick marks of who succeeded in what category.

About twelve seconds in, I noticed a profound lack of quiet.

"Let's do this in a calm fashion," I instructed, taking the cup and demonstrating how a gentleman might play Yahtzee. They were intrigued.

"My turn," shouted a boy. He took the cup, shook it violently, and tossed the dice across the table. He was pleased with the results, which wound up on the floor and under the table. His roll was good for his score but bad for my ears.

This went on for a while, a lot longer than I remember Yahtzee ever being. And while it was a lot of fun, I found myself having a constant tug-of-war between enjoying the moment with my brood of cubs and telling them, in a steady, loving tone, to be quiet.

My husband tells me part of the problem is that I'm not mean enough—that I don't always speak the language my boys understand. I'm starting to catch on that if I say something with too much calm in my voice, the message is totally lost. Unless, of course, I go over to the dark side of calm and conduct myself with such quiet tranquility that my boys suspect I am about to snap—only then will they calm down.

That's what happened around the end of the game that night. I had reached my limit and felt like I couldn't handle one more roll. The sound of the dice tumbling across the coffee table seemed more like giant boulders being tossed at my head. I was checking my watch every ten seconds and developing a twitch.

We made it through the game, but I had to tally the score the next morning. My reserves were all used up, my abilities to act loving and sane were gone. I hope my boys won't go into therapy for the times we played board games and Mommy nutted up. That would defeat the point of all this family togetherness.

The real lesson to be learned is that families like mine should definitely enjoy playing games together, but will likely have more fun doing things that appeal to the majority of the group.

"Two of my favorite things," sighed Ethan one evening as we spent time together in the backyard, "fire and hatchets."

They do know what they like. I give them credit for that.

Pellet Gun Control

It is early afternoon and the boys are discussing big plans, some gizmo they are hoping to build that I'm pretty sure will end in bodily harm coming to one of them.

After this many years with this many boys, I am getting a bit jumpy. I don't have a tic, not yet anyway, but it's like I have this built-in radar that picks up even the slightest hint of boyish engineering. As soon as the drawing papers emerge, so do I.

Sometimes, but not often, there is nothing to worry about.

"I have a great idea," I once heard a boy declare, "and I'm gonna need a bucket."

That sent me running in his direction, because our track record with great ideas and buckets is not that great. In the past, it has ended in bottles being shot at with a BB gun (with the bucket to "contain" the mess) as well as precious items being dropped from a second-story bedroom window (with the bucket to "contain" the mess).

That time, the boy was only planning on icing down some drinks. Who knew they could be so civil?

On this afternoon, however, I overhear that they have *plans*. I immediately tune in to their discussion, listening intently. After a minute, I decide to offer some guidelines. I point out that they need to think through what will happen when they (*insert questionable behavior here*) or how they think it will feel if they get hit by (*insert dangerous materials here*).

"What do you think the outcome will be?" I prod.

"Ah, Mom," says one of the boys, "you always think of all the detailed stuff."

No mother sets out to be a killjoy. It just comes with the job.

I try hard to be open-minded. Not in a "tolerance, they'll figure this out on their own" kind of way; that's a mentality I can't afford. But sometimes I want to be open to the idea that maybe my boys can handle trying a certain activity or that I should allow them to have a certain toy/weapon. Perhaps I don't always give them enough credit, but (as is more often the case) perhaps I give them too much.

Each Christmas season, the boys draw a brother's name to give him a "secret" gift on Christmas morning. A few days before Christmas, I take the boys shopping for the one shopping trip of the year that they actually look forward to. There is a set amount to spend, and they try to secretly pick out a gift while no one is looking.

One year, in a moment of weakness, I let them buy each other air-soft guns, those plastic guns that shoot out plastic pellets. Because I put a fairly low dollar cap on our spending, the boys were forced to buy the lowest-end guns on the market.

They were ecstatic. They could not believe their good fortune.

"You're really going to let us buy these?" they kept asking, and of course by then the secret aspect of the day was gone. The level of excitement kept growing, and I began to wonder if I should reconsider, because the boys were so amazed by my decision. For several years the boys had been asking me about buying these cheap weapons, and every time I was able to put it off. I kept the solid vision in my mind of what an eye being shot out actually looks like. I don't really know, but I've seen enough Chuck Norris movies to have an idea.

Over time, however, I had started to see the boys display little moments of sanity, times when they sat and carved with a pocketknife and did harm to no one. Times when they were shooting the BB gun and aimed at the target only. In fact, they had gotten into the regular habit of handling these situations in a responsible and proper fashion.

So there we were, that Christmas season, and I was feeling generous and safe.

"Yes," I assured them, "you can indeed buy these guns for each other."

The only stipulation was that each boy needed to wrap the gift for his brother, and that there would be no opening the presents until Christmas morning.

It was almost more than they could bear.

Finally, the five or six days passed and Christmas morning came. The boys opened all the gifts, including and most especially the gifts to each other. Those cheap little weapons were the highlight of the morning, outshining months of online shopping and numerous trips to the sports emporium.

Out they went to play, and sure enough after mere moments in the backyard, someone got hurt. An unsuspecting victim took a pellet to the delicate area just outside the eye. Thus began a major overhaul to our safety system. Paul and I had to come up with even more specific rules and regulations regarding pellet gun usage than had previously been stated.

I was relaying this story to my brother-in-law a few weeks

Essentials of a Boy's Life 🏈

later, telling him all about how much the boys love these guns and how long they went without any problems.

"Yup," I told him, "it took about twelve minutes for someone to get an eye injury and the fun to end."

"Wow," he said in amazement, "that's a lot longer than I would have guessed."

Fine Arts

It started as such a good idea: exposure to art, learning, having fun. But that's not how it turned out.

It was the end of a long, hot summer. We stopped in to visit a friend and found the family hard at work painting canvas with oils. They had been inspired by a recent trip to the National Gallery of Art in our nation's capital.

"What a great idea," I remarked. I decided that a hands-on art project would be just the ticket for our end-of-the-summer ennui.

A few days later, the boys and I headed to the local art supply store. My friend had found oils that washed with water, she said, and paired with cheap paintbrushes, their end results were creative and lovely.

At the store with a shopping cart full of boys, I grabbed the first set of oils that matched my friend's description. Each boy then picked out the canvas he wanted, and we were back on the road before anyone could say "aisle full of scissors."

Once home, we broke out the supplies. It was a tad complicated and slightly harried as I ran for water and doled out paint. But eventually we got settled, and each boy began to work on his masterpiece.

The problems started soon after. One boy got terribly agitated when, after sinking his brush into the water, the paint did not wash off. In fact, the brush seemed to actually repel the water. The other boys soon realized the same frustration. Whatever paint it was that my friend used, I thought, this isn't it.

My stomach felt a little funny all of a sudden, and I had the sickening suspicion that we got oils, but not the kind that washes with water.

Fortunately, we had enough cheap brushes to reach for a new one as needed, and I figured once that option dried up, painting time was over. That was the best I could offer.

Ethan fell into a rhythm and finished his "still life with house." He was quick and neat and soon out the door. A few minutes later, Charlie completed a very nice abstract and followed his brother outside. That left two boys still working at the table, both of whom were growing increasingly frustrated.

"Whhhhhyyyy," began Elliott, "can't I sign my naaamme???" The harder he tried, the more exasperated he became.

Augie, meanwhile, managed to get several clumps of orange paint on his hands. I decided to throw him in the tub. We left his exaggerated Pollack to dry and headed to the bathroom. I filled the tub and plopped him in.

While Augie soaked, I started to scrub my own hands that, in the course of undressing my boy, had gotten covered with orange-speckled paint as well.

As I began to scrub, it became frighteningly clear that this wasn't effective at all. After about two minutes of massive suds and hot water, my hands looked like the victim of a nuclear accident. The orange splotches turned into orange gloves, complete with fingertip-to-wrist coverage and a shiny glow.

Meanwhile, Augie was hunched over in the tub, which now looked like it was filled with radioactive waste. What was once warm, clear water was now a murky soup. There was an orange ring all around the tub, and somehow my boy's entire face was orange. He had several streaks of orange paint in his hair, as well as every other area of his body his hand had even grazed in the last five minutes.

I started to panic. Scrubbing, panting, thinking. We were scheduled to visit his preschool the next day, and one look at Augie's orange glow sent a sharp pain to my chest.

Preschool orientation had been a few days earlier, and it was there I sent shock waves through the classroom when, after the teacher asked for donations of castoff dress-ups, I wondered aloud if that included weapons.

There were several audible gasps.

"No," whispered two mothers, "no weapons!"

Showing up with a glow-in-the-dark halfling might not win me any more friends.

Just then, I had a lightbulb moment, likely inspired by all that nausea and dread. Makeup remover! A while ago, I had reluctantly bought a bottle from my Mary Kay representative after she convinced me that wiping my eyes until they were raw was not the best way to remove mascara.

I grabbed the bottle from my medicine cabinet and began to massage small amounts onto my son's forehead and cheeks.

Like magic, the glow began to subside, and after only fifteen minutes, my son was almost entirely back to normal.

For weeks after that, I would find a dab of the oil paint here or there, a small spot that had somehow traveled through the house waiting to be discovered and cleaned. It was a good lesson for so many reasons, but mostly I learned this: listen to your Mary Kay consultant. Her selling skills could save your life.

Charlie, whimpering: "Elliott took my cape and didn't even give me a REPLACEMENT!"

Essentials of a Boy's Life 🏈

GEAR I RECOMMEND FOR LIFE WITH BOYS:

- One old couch. This will save on wear and tear of the good couch, which I suggest you keep in another part of the house where your boys are not. The old couch can be used for a variety of activities, including but not limited to: the foundation for an awesome fort; the platform for amazing front and back flips: hiding behind; part of an obstacle course; the occasional nap; and (least likely) a place to sit quietly and read.
- Blankets. These will come in handy for building forts; stuffing down pants and into shirts to look like musclemen; wrapping up an unsuspecting brother; covering the top of a large box to make a spaceship; morphing into a large worm; providing cover for the occasional nap; making a palette for a spend-the-night in big brothers' room.
- Legos. The only toy you'll ever need. In almost all cases, these guarantee hours of uninterrupted downtime. Dump a container of Legos and see who can create the biggest and baddest spaceship. Also useful for creating crime-stopping robots and miniature guns.
- Access to a large tree. The ideal, of course, is that you will have a tree of your own. If not, work out something with a neighbor. Our best trees are actually next door in Gramma and Papa's backyard. One tree includes a fort made by Papa and the uncles. Research has shown that trees are also good for the environment, but we like them even more for climbing and gathering sticks to build stuff.
- Twine and/or fishing line. For tying up the sticks and turning them into fishing poles, swords, daggers, and bows and arrows. Most of these endeavors start out sanctioned by Mom and somehow go downhill from there.
- Duct tape. Enough said.
- White Hanes T-shirts, and many of them. Inexpensive, easy to bleach, and when bleaching doesn't work, easy to ditch because they cost next to nothing.
- Blue jeans. The pants that are always in season. Perfect for climbing

trees, hikes in the woods, and those times when your boy is being dragged across the backyard while holding onto his brother's speeding bike.

- Wooden blocks. Work as a fortress for army guys, LEGO guys, plastic animals, and action figures. Also good for wannabe architects and overlords.
- A good pediatrician, preferably one who also has a bunch of boys.
- A tattletale. Sadly, I don't have one of these, but I often think about how great it would be to have access to one.

7

The Sweet Side

Introduction to My World

The phone rings, I answer. It's our friend, calling from his cell phone. He just drove by, and the boys, all four of them, are standing on top of the truck in our driveway.

"One of the boys is holding some kind of a bat," he relays, and I can tell he is watching them in the mirror as he passes our house. "He's holding a bat and whacking the top of the cab."

He is laughing a little, our friend, but I can tell he is intrigued and possibly unnerved. I would have felt the same.

Before I was a mother to a bunch of boys, I was easily awed by other families. I was quick to assess the behavior of children, quick to raise an eyebrow at children who yelled or ran or stood on the top of a truck and hit it with a bat. Extremely bad parenting, I would note. So subpar.

But then I became a parent. Suddenly I was living in the challenge that parenting really is. You can discipline and talk all day long, but so often you deal with stuff as it happens. I never told the boys not to climb on the top of the truck and hit it with a bat—I guess I never thought to.

I thank our friend, hang up the phone, and walk to the window. Sure enough, the truck is swarming with little boys.

Boys in capes, with plastic bats, wearing masks, beating the top of the truck with all their might.

Welcome to My World.

Several years ago, when boy number four turned one, I became acutely aware of how my life was changing. Up to that point, even with four boys, there was not the herd I have now. Back then, it was four little boys who played hard, who dressed up and built shops and ran all day—but it was still on a relatively small scale, these antics of theirs.

Back then, a fort needed only one blanket. A tower was made out of big LEGO blocks, and it was a simple structure that stretched in one direction—toward the sky. Dress-up meant donning a cowboy hat and boots. Also, to my advantage, there was still a lot of parallel play—four boys playing alongside each other, not fully aware of the wealth of adventure that lingered just beside them.

Then, slowly, each boy outgrew the phase of a singular existence. Over time, each one discovered his surroundings, and that included those brothers he had been sharing life with. The more this happened, the more things changed, and one day, I realized I was about to begin an adventure much more grand than I had planned.

One late afternoon in fall, I look out my kitchen window. Moving slowly through the backyard is a small tribe. The wagon has become a throne on wheels. It bears the archery target, a dense cardboard box, now covered with blankets. My five-year-old is kneeling on top, his hands on the tops of his legs. He is staring straight ahead. A blanket covers his head and back.

Behind him, a brother marches slowly, carrying a spear. It is a very tall walking stick culled from the yard. Another brother walks in front, gently pulling the throne to its destination.

The group walks deliberately, staring ahead, taking the leader where he wills.

I watch as they round a corner of the yard and move slowly out of my view.

That this is a normal part of my daily life still makes me smile. I hope it always does.

How I Do It

When people ask me how I do it, I am quick to tell them one thing: I have help.

It's not necessarily live-in childcare or a full-time maid service. I have those things, of course, but I call that woman Me.

What I have is good friends, real friends whom I can be totally honest with. I don't need a lot of these women—you really just need a handful, maybe even just one or two. What's important is to have these people to go to and be totally, completely honest. You need women you don't feel threatened by or in competition with, a person who has your back—and maybe a little piece of your heart as well.

I have good friends who know just about everything about me—women I can call and ask: is this kind of behavior normal? These friendships were invaluable to me early on, as my boys were emerging from the tiny babies they once were. When the questions and conflicts arose, and I began to realize that the way boys deal with anger and frustration is generally the opposite of what my nature says to do, I worked up the courage to ask a few friends about their experience.

To me, that kind of wisdom and advice cannot be bought. It is the fruit of investing your time with people you trust.

I love talking to women who are in the same boat I am now, but I also want to talk to women who have already raised boys, preferably lots of them, and lived to tell the tale. I have five brothers, and my mom offers a lot of wisdom. And I speak to her friends too, women whom I have known since I was a girl. Those are the women who can remind me that some of the things I'm worked up about today do not matter in the big picture. Or conversely, they remind me to fight the good fight—that yes, some of these seemingly insignificant details are in fact worth the effort.

Today

Today we are going to get flu shots. It could be painful—maybe even for the boys.

Today I'm thinking about Christmas decorations, about getting the tree this weekend and making sure I have all the empty boxes back in the attic before the weekend is over.

Today I'm preoccupied with a party I'm hosting. I know the guests will never see the inside of my closet; why do I sweat the small stuff?

But today I'm also sweating the less-small stuff—because while the guests won't see the inside of my closet, they'll probably notice those shoeprints on the wall. Those I should sweat.

Today I feel (slightly) guilty that last night, when a boy was going on and on about how life is so tough because dinner is never what he wants and his lunches stink too, I opened the phone book to a random name. And I asked that boy if he'd rather go live with, hmmm, let's see . . . Ferguson. Do you think Mr. Ray Ferguson might cook something you'd rather eat? And suddenly that boy was pretty happy with the menu around here. So then I assured him I'd never give him away, even if he doesn't gush about my cooking.

Today, every time I think about writing, all I want to say is, "My boys are amazing! I can't get enough of these kids!" But then I start to think that's goofy. So I hide those sentiments among all this other minutiae.

(My boys are amazing. I can't get enough of these kids.)

Embracing Who I Am

So much goes into our makeup as a family, including my interests and my husband's interests.

One Christmas I decided to make stained-glass cookies.

"We need to do this," I told myself, lamenting the fact that no one seemed to care that we hadn't spent all of Advent baking in the kitchen.

I called one of the boys into the kitchen, dragging him away from some other project he was doing with his brothers.

"I'm not the best man for this job," he said after a minute. "I think you need someone with smaller hands."

Later that day, still laboring under a false sense of domestic duty, we strung cranberries and popcorn. But I was busy in the kitchen finishing up the stained-glass cookies (with my smaller hands), and despite getting to handle the sharp needles, the boys grew weary of finagling temperamental popcorn kernels.

In the end, I learned what they want from me: my chocolate chip cookies and maybe (if no one is looking) a kiss on the lips.

"Do you know why these cookies are the best?" asked Augie. "It's because you made them."

We are driving in the car, Paul and me and our boys. We are listening to a lovely and sweet song, a song about courage and love and the depths of our understanding of God.

The song ends and the car is quiet for a moment. I'm thinking about my relationship with God, my view of the world, and how my own life experiences often limit what I understand about God's love for me.

That everyone else is so still, I am sure, means we are all similarly moved.

After a minute, Elliott breaks the silence.

"Daddy," he asks in a gentle voice, "what team was Wilt Chamberlain on when he retired?"

Growing Pains

Boys grow up. I'm starting to learn this. While those early years with lots of little toddlers were mostly fun but also often excruciating, we have eased into years with more laughter than tears (instead of equal parts).

As the boys get older, there are still plenty of challenges, but those challenges have changed. The same physical requirements are not demanded of me, because the bulk of our crew is older and more independent. And while they're not necessarily wiser, they are mostly learning.

I first realized this one Christmas break when, after two weeks of having the boys home with me, I was sad to see them go back to school. I will miss you, I told them, and they assured me they'd come home as soon as the bell rang, right after school.

Before I got too sentimental and forgot a little distance is healthy for us all, one of the boys shot a Nerf gun at the newspaper I was reading. It broke through the paper, tearing into my shoulder and scaring the crud out of me.

"Who did that!" I bellowed, whipping the paper into my lap. The culprit, staring at me from across the room, was trying to conjure an excuse.

"I asked him if I should shoot," Charlie said, pointing to his older brother, "and he said I should do it."

And that is when I did it—I pulled out a classic and

asked him about the bridge and everyone else and what he would do if everyone else said to jump. I tried for something more original, but it was no use. The bridge is just so hard to beat.

Charlie assured me he would never jump off a bridge, no matter what. And I remember giving my mom that same answer. The problem here, though, is that I bet my mother believed me. With these boys, I don't think I can afford to do the same.

For as much as I joke about my life with all these boys, and talk about how crazy it is and how wild they are, and laugh about who will get stuck with me when they get old, I am almost always acutely aware of the honor and privilege it is to be raising my sons.

These boys in my care are tomorrow's men, and like parents the world over, Paul and I will have a direct impact on the future through the way we raise our children.

Yes, it would be nice to have quiet offspring, to be surrounded by humans who are essentially like me, only shorter. That would certainly make my job easier. "Let's all sit and look at magazines for a while," I'd say, and we would spend the afternoon in glorious leisure.

Instead I am outside chasing a toddler who is hardwired to climb on everything in his sights, who is immediately gunning for another tall object the moment he is removed from the current one.

I can certainly bring a magazine outside to read, but I will most likely not be joined by my boys. They will be busy digging in the yard, or climbing the fort, or having a contest to see who can make the most free throws in a row.

One afternoon the boys were in the driveway playing basketball.

"Let's shoot some hoops," I said to them. "Let's play Horse."

"Actually we're playing Pig," said Elliott. "But you could play Horse. Or maybe Water Buffalo."

I spend my days trying to find a balance in protecting my boys from the dangers of the world while letting them discover the beauty of it. I want to let them run and jump and climb and build, without crashing and burning in the process.

The scary part of being a female raising males, or maybe just being a parent in general, is that I have to guide and mold the nature of these boys without working against it. It is not in my nature to run screaming through the backyard while carrying a large stick. But it is in the nature of my boys, and I don't want to squelch who they are simply because I don't always understand it.

I think I have loosened the leash just a bit. The old me, the mother I was before I had children, wouldn't have allowed some of the things I allow now. Not necessarily with what shows we watch or what language we use—there are plenty of issues I stand firm on.

The changes are centered more on the adventures I permit my boys to have. When we go to the ocean, I don't want them to go past their ankles, but it cannot always be that way.

As they grow and bloom and spread their wings, I have to do the same. I have to keep up with them, while allowing them to be who God created them to be.

The Easy Life

I cannot tell you the number of people who come up to me when we are out in public, who pull me aside and whisper to me that having all boys is simple—that boys are so much easier than girls. I hear this a lot, and some days I take comfort in that fact.

Some days, however, it draws a different response from me.

If it's so easy, I wonder, why am I counting down the minutes to Happy Hour? Why do I sometimes find myself yelling? Why are there moments when the last thing in the world I want to do is get to the bottom of why your brother whacked you for no good reason? Because surely there is a good reason, even though of course we don't whack each other.

"With girls," people will tell me, "it's all so emotional. And things are never what they seem."

It's true that with boys, what you see is what you get. I love and appreciate that about boys. I appreciate it even more when we're in the privacy of our own home.

What is incredibly challenging about boys, my boys anyway, is that when they have an issue, they'd like to deal with it right then, if you please. I once had a boy elbow his brother right in the middle of Mass because the brother had nudged him first. This needs to wait until later, I whispered to the pair, sweat beading on my forehead. They seemed baffled that I would suggest putting this off until a more appropriate time. What, they seemed to wonder, does that even mean?

Boys are also less inclined to linger. They don't seem compelled to stay right by me when we are out—they are not afraid of getting lost. In fact, that might be kinda fun.

One summer afternoon, a friend and I took our children to the local science museum. She had her five children (two girls, three boys), and I had my four boys. This was pre-Henry, and long enough ago that no one was all that big and properly independent.

We arrived at the museum and had a long, drawn-out pep talk in the parking lot. It was there I went over ad nauseum the importance of staying right by me, where I droned on and on and belabored the point and maybe even threatened loss of privilege and food to those who got too far ahead.

Ten minutes later, we walked inside the museum and my boys disappeared immediately. Gone from my side, out of my sight, zipping through the exhibits like monkeys on speed.

After the fourth or fifth time of reeling them in, I started to get discouraged. I wasn't giving up, mind you. But I was certainly tired of having to try so hard.

Right around this time, another friend walked by. This father was there with his five daughters, all of whom were dutifully holding onto a piece of his clothing as they toured the sights.

"How do you do that?" I asked, while looking around for even a remote sign of my boys.

He explained that he had instructed the girls to stay nearby, and that if they ran off, they would have to run laps or do pushups when they got home. That sounded like a good idea for about a second, until I realized my boys would take that as some kind of incentive, and not as punishment.

After the dad left, I turned to my friend with a look of frustration and possibly dismay.

"How can having boys be easier?" I asked. "I just don't see it."

"It's not," she told me. And she admitted that to her, boys were harder.

At least in this situation, I know she was right. I was living proof that even if girls are emotional and conniving, at least they stay put.

Family Charms

Some weekends are better than others. Some Sundays can be particularly rough for us if we end up just lazing around doing nothing. For our family, doing nothing often leads to nothing good.

When we operate out of this knowledge and understanding, however, our days can be glorious.

One Sunday afternoon, we loaded up the boys and headed down to the river. For two hours, we frolicked and played. We all walked on the rocks and crossed the entire river. We waded in the water, jumped in the water, swam in the water—and simply enjoyed an adventure together.

I told my husband later that evening, as we shared a family walk, how that kind of day really feeds the souls of our boys. I can tell. As we walked from one side of the river to the other (and then back again), I saw a beautiful camaraderie among our sons. I noted the way they were acting and how they treated each other, and it was evidence of what this kind of adventure does for them. Being outdoors in nature, free to explore and live life—this fulfills a vital part of who they are, perhaps as children, perhaps as male children.

With these sons of mine, there are going to be certain family activities that will just click better for us. Shopping is something we endure, eating is something we enjoy—but adventure, being in the great outdoors, pushing ourselves and exploring the world around us—that is something we live for.

Fine Living, Indoor and Out

Paul and I were discussing plans for our yard one evening, trying to decide where we could put a white picket fence that wouldn't interfere with the constant basketball game going on in the driveway or with the frequent bicycle trips around the house.

"Why don't we just put some kind of structure right here?" I explain, showing my husband where we could install something that would meet our needs without disrupting boy-living at its finest. I was getting excited, imagining a screen of confederate jasmine and fragrant clematis.

"We could do that," says Charlie, "or what about a trampoline? Maybe a trampoline on top of a trampoline, with a zip-line going over it."

It's not that they want to sabotage my view, I tell myself. We just have different standards of beauty. My standards involve a love of lush greenery and of not seeing my boys get their necks broken. My poor sons are stuck with a freelance writer of a mother who once did a story on how trampolines are not recommended by the American Pediatric Association and has never looked back.

I return to my thoughts of flora and fauna, to my hopes of having a yard that is more *Southern Living* and less *Huckleberry Finn*. I want to be that rare creature who somehow has a home that is filled with boys as well as the essence of creative beauty.

My job gets harder every single day.

"Don't you shoot hoops in my cashmere gloves," I find

myself hollering out the back door one afternoon. Despite their abject disinterest in fashion and dressing nice, my sons are somehow inherently aware of the treasure that is this pair of gloves, this pair of brand-new, creamy white cashmere gloves I received that Christmas from my sister.

"Where's the duct tape?" asks Elliott one afternoon. He comes to me wearing my gloves.

"You're not duct-taping my cashmere glove onto your arm," I tell him, taking the delicate objects to place under lock and key.

It's not all rough-and-tumble, though plenty of it is. Boys certainly have a sweet side that is irresistibly charming and delicious.

One afternoon Augie walks into the kitchen, his cupped palms filled with silky loose petals.

"I couldn't get a whole flower off the tree," he says, offering the handful to me.

"Thank you," I tell him, leaning down for a kiss. He smells like the essence of little boy, fresh air from outdoors infused with sweat. He leans up for a peck before heading back outdoors.

On my jewelry box, there is a tiny handmade flower that I keep perched on the edge. It is a rose, fashioned out of a twist tie, a gift from a boy whose heart was overflowing with love for me.

It is certainly a mutual admiration society, even on the days when child rearing is grungier and louder than I would have imagined. These boys are the jewels in my very rustic crown, a crown I wear with a complicated mixture of pride and humility.

Boy at dinner: "Wow, this is actually pretty good. I guess I won't throw up after all."

Oh-So-Tiny Acts of Love

In addition to handfuls of flower petals and twist-tie roses, my boys have other ways they show me their love. My days are filled with tiny gestures, sometimes much tinier than others, as the boys strive to articulate how much they care.

Every morning in the cold-weather months, one of the boys will go out to the car and turn on my seat warmer. When I get in the car a few minutes later, I am greeted by hospitably warm leather.

"Thank you for warming my seat," I'll say, and I can tell that the boy responsible is quite pleased with his gesture.

Someone thought of me in advance—my son anticipated my need—and this means as much to me as a hundred grand, showy gestures.

One day I walked by the bathroom just as my eight-year-old was finishing up. The door was open of course, and I happened to glimpse just as he put the lid down and then flushed the toilet.

"Thank you so much for doing that," I gushed.

"It was nothing," he said. But I know he does it for me. There is nothing else that would compel him.

The boys compliment me on my housekeeping skills. "You're a good mopper," a boy once told me. This comment carried me for days. When we are hiking, there will always be one boy who turns to check on me if I fall behind, waiting patiently until I catch up. It won't necessarily be the entire pack of them, but it only takes one act of kindness to remind me I am loved.

The boys thank me for the meals I cook and seem grateful when their favorite basketball shorts are somehow clean and waiting for them every afternoon. And of course, they are happy to the point of tears and hugs when I stock the pantry with the foods they love—because that is the language they speak, and they want to say they love me right back.

Battles are won and lost in the million details of a day, and when I feel love in these tiny ways, I am reminded over and over that boys are indeed fearfully and wonderfully made. They might swing from the rafters and dream of jumping off the roof, but they are also incredibly thoughtful and loving and have a tender side that will occasionally reveal itself.

You just have to be looking, to be paying attention to the small things so you are sure not to miss it.

Firstborn Son

It was the evening of our oldest son's birthday, and for some reason I was clipping everyone's toenails. For tasks of a hygienic nature, I have learned to strike while the iron is hot. A birthday is no exception.

When I came to the birthday boy's feet, I was amazed. They had grown overnight.

I looked at those toes, and my thoughts went back to the first time I ever saw them, back when they were tiny little toes on tiny little feet.

It was a very early autumn morning, and there I sat holding my firstborn son. I had wanted a boy so badly, and here he was. At that moment, as I counted his fingers and toes and looked at his perfectly formed lips, I'm sure I had no inkling of the joy that was to come. I was just glad he was here, safe and sound, and that the act of giving birth was over.

The first days and weeks of having a baby are a blur, and when I watch the videos, it is obvious I had no idea what I was doing.

At one point, as we were preparing to leave the hospital, my dad taped me getting ready to dress the baby for the first time. On the tape, I ready Ethan's outfit, smoothing it on the hospital bed, eyeing this tiny baby lying next to it. I smooth the clothes again, look at the baby, clear my throat, and then reluctantly dive in. I remember being concerned about pulling his tiny leg through the clothing. Would even the slightest pressure cause it to break? I was so unsure.

And here we are, a few years later, and this tiny baby is now resting his enormous foot on my knee. It was just yesterday, I marvel, that this foot fit in my palm.

My boys all love pointing out how much they have grown, and how pretty soon they will be as tall as I am.

They're right, of course. I look at my oldest son, and I realize that day in the hospital is a lifetime ago. That day, I met this tiny, precious, unknown bundle who I knew would bring me joy. I just had no idea how much.

That birthday evening, after the toenails had been clipped and everyone had gone to bed, I snuck up into my oldest boy's room. I sat on his bed, smoothed his hair, and stared at his face as he slept.

I thought about the wonderful celebrations of the day. I thought about the fun we had as a family and with friends. I wondered if my son enjoyed all the festivities, and if he was happy with his party and his gifts—how he got exactly what he wanted, including that Ultimate Lightsaber and the pocketknife with multiple features.

As I sat there watching him sleep, I wondered if my boy would ever realize the depth of my love for him. I realized that the greatest gift my husband and I will ever give this boy—all of our boys—is our unconditional, undying love, to them and to each other. All the plastic and metal and paper will come and go, but this joy I have from simply looking at these precious creatures—and realizing the depth of God's love for me through them—this is a love that I hope will stay with my children the rest of their lives.

The Future Is Wild

We have a game I purchased a while back, something that fosters communication among the family. It comes beautifully packaged in an acrylic cube and is full of cards that have specific topics to discuss as a family.

Don't get me wrong—we talk plenty. But sometimes I would like dinner conversations to revolve around concepts and topics that are more encompassing than who has scored the most points ever in the history of the NBA, or what Amazonian snake can eat the biggest pig.

One afternoon Augie pulled out a card from the stack and asked if I wanted to have a discussion. I told him I would be happy to.

"What one thing," he started to read, "would you like to know about the future?"

I sat quietly, thinking about the question. I looked at my sweet boy staring back at me as he waited for my answer. His blond hair swept to the side, his head barely sticking above the table. He leaned forward and watched.

I thought about the future and all it holds—all the joy and excitement, the adventures we will share, the fun times yet to come. I thought about my boys getting older and our family evolving into a group that will enjoy each other more and more as the years pass.

I eyed my blond-headed boy, and I realized that one day he

will be big enough to have adventures all on his own. Slowly this boy will get bigger, bigger than me, and probably bigger than his dad. *One day*, I thought, as I looked into his bright green eyes, *you will move out of my house and you will no longer be this little boy who is just sitting here hanging on my every word*.

Then I thought about the heartaches and sadness that life will inevitably bring. *I hope it will never be more than he can handle*, I thought, looking at my boy, and for a split second it was more than I could bear. *What if something terrible happens?* I thought. *How could I ever survive?*

"I don't think I want to know anything about the future," I finally answered, my chest suddenly feeling heavy and tight. "I'd rather just enjoy this moment right now."

"Well, I'd want to know when the first flying car was invented," said my son, now gazing dreamily into the distance, "and also if that car will have a dinosaur claw attached to the front."

"Do you know where my favorite place on earth is?" my son asked as we pulled into the driveway.

"Where's that?" I responded.

"Right here, at our house."

Rachel Balducci is a writer and the mother of five lively boys. She is a newspaper columnist and a former staff writer for the *Augusta Chronicle*. She has been published in numerous magazines, including *Good Housekeeping*, *Faith and Family*, and *The Word Among Us*, and she was a featured writer in *Blessings: Reflections on Gratitude, Love, and What Makes Us Happy* (Heart Press).

Rachel's website, www.testosterhome.net, has been nominated for several awards.